Giving Up Is Unforgivable

Giving Up Is Unforgivable

A MANUAL FOR

KEEPING

A DEMOCRACY

Joyce Vance

DUTTON

DUTTON

An imprint of Penguin Random House LLC
1745 Broadway, New York, NY 10019
penguinrandomhouse.com

DUTTON and the D colophon are registered trademarks of
Penguin Random House LLC.

Book design by Angie Boutin

LIBRARY OF CONGRESS CATALOGING-IN-PUBLICATION DATA
has been applied for.

ISBN 9798217178117 (hardcover)
ISBN 9798217178124 (ebook)

Printed in the United States of America
1st Printing

The authorized representative in the EU for product safety and compliance
is Penguin Random House Ireland, Morrison Chambers, 32 Nassau Street,
Dublin D02 YH68, Ireland, https://eu-contact.penguin.ie.

To Bob, for bringing home my German shepherd, Bella,
who sat patiently by my side while I wrote this book

Contents

Giving Up Is Unforgivable

Introduction

Did you, too, O friend, suppose democracy was only for elections, for politics, and for a party name? I say democracy is only of use there that it may pass on and come to its flower and fruit in manners, in the highest forms of interaction between men, and their beliefs—in religion, literature, colleges, and schools—democracy in all public and private life.

—Walt Whitman

Could I have picked a worse time to write a book about saving democracy? It certainly felt like the answer was no as I embarked on this project. In January 2025, Donald Trump was inaugurated for a second term as the president of the United States of America. In its first few weeks, the new administration spewed out anti-democratic moves with overwhelming force and velocity. This should not have come as a surprise to anyone. The intention was laid out clearly during Trump's first administration, in his campaign promises, and in the conservative blueprint for his second term in office, Project 2025. But the speed, the scope, and the utter lawlessness of the efforts caught people off guard. The cavalier disregard for American norms and the abandon with which the new administration acted felt like a bad nightmare we couldn't wake up from. In those early weeks, it was hard to keep up with everything that was happening, let alone figure out how we were going to hold on to democracy.

There is a world of difference between a president who makes lawful policy choices that you or I may disagree with and a president who brazenly exceeds the powers that Article II of the Constitution assigns to the office he temporarily holds. The former is a matter for the ballot box, while the latter demands a functioning Article I branch of government (Congress) and a functioning Article III branch (the courts), along with a free press, to hold him in check.

Elections have consequences. A new president sets priorities, policy, and the course of government. But the new Trump administration was showing an utter lack of regard for charting that course in a lawful manner. Straight out of the gate, Trump fired inspectors general in federal agencies without complying with legal requirements that he first give notice to Congress. It seemed like a small thing to some, but when faced with two choices, one clearly lawful, he chose the other, the one that pushed the limits of presidential power.

Then Trump attempted to remove birthright citizenship from the Constitution with the stroke of a pen, instead of initiating the process required to amend the Constitution. Next was the Department of Government Efficiency (DOGE), and then deportations conducted without due process. Government employees who had worked on investigations involving January 6 or had looked into Trump himself were fired. Law firms and universities were subjected to executive orders that demanded their obedience if they wanted to stay in existence. As pro-democracy lawyers began to litigate these issues, a still more serious concern came to the forefront: What would the Trump administration do if it suffered a loss in court? Might it simply refuse to follow the law?

As I began this book, the future path was unknowable. Early on, I tore up a lot of pages because everything I wrote seemed to go quickly out of date. I watched (and wrote) as Elon Musk performed his charade of finding fraud and waste in government at DOGE, and while it seemed clear to me that this was not a lawful effort to serve the American people, it was far from certain where the issues would end up as they worked their way through the courts. The same was true for Trump's impoundment of congressionally authorized expenditures, his efforts to fire agency heads and federal employees alike, the politicization of the Department of Justice, and the destruction of the Department of Education.

Then, about a month into writing, I realized what I was missing in the deluge. It had become easy to see where we were weak. It was more difficult to see where we were strong. The question that began to present itself was whether the fundamental values that underlie our system of government, the American democracy so many of us believe in, are sturdy enough to withstand these challenges. The rule of law was being stretched to its limits, but it was not completely broken.

Our country has struggled through difficult times using the system of government and laws created by the founders. Though it is far from perfect, the system that was born with the taint of racism and misogyny has also proven itself capable of improvement, even when it is incremental. It is a system that is capable of change and progress when threatened.

We have the capacity to do so much more, to *be* more, to include an ever-expanding number of people in the promise of America. That's what frightens Trump and his ilk: the idea of a more perfect, diverse union. As Dr. Martin Luther King Jr. taught, we have the potential to become a country where the content of a person's character and not the color of their skin—or who they love, where they come from, what god they worship or not—determines their prospects in society. That vision of an inclusive America is threatening to some people. They are afraid of us.

With that awareness I realized that I was free to write. Because I wanted to write about how to save the Republic, sure, but also about the future. About what we can do if we renew our commitment to democracy, reinvigorate civics education, and resist those who would drag us back to less enlightened times. Progress may not be linear, but that doesn't mean we can't look forward beyond these difficult years we are living through and prepare to regain our America.

It's inherently challenging to write about the present moment in America because the crisis is unfolding at breakneck speed. Nonetheless, I've tried because it seemed too important to let it go. A book must necessarily lag in the news cycle by a number of months. I hope that the big picture perspective the medium allows is worth some trade-off in up-to-the-minute timeliness.

We'll proceed like this: Chapter 1 outlines the parameters of our present constitutional crisis. Chapter 2 is about institutions: How they were designed to work and how we can strengthen them. Chapter 3 answers a question I am alarmed to hear more and more often these days: Why have a democracy at all? Chapter 4 draws out the lessons we can learn from the Founding Fathers, literature, and American history (especially the Civil War and the Civil Rights Movement) as we confront the current menace. Chapter 5 goes deep on the act that is the foundation of our democracy: Voting. And chapter 6, the most important chapter of the book, spells out what *you* can do, and what we can achieve together.

THERE'S A WONDERFUL STORY ABOUT BEN FRANKLIN. AS IT'S TOLD, he was walking out of Independence Hall after the Constitutional Convention of 1787 and a woman called out, "Well, Doctor, what have we got? A republic or a monarchy?" Franklin is said to have responded, "A republic . . . if you can keep it."

The challenge was clear. The work of democracy is the people's work. It is the challenge we have to take up now.

I'd like to be a part of keeping the Republic. That's why I started my Substack, "Civil Discourse," on June 7, 2022. I wasn't sure anyone would read it, but that was okay, because I was mostly writing for myself, trying to sort out how I felt about some of the most pressing issues we faced. Despite the serious challenges, I believed there was still reason for optimism. Civics education pays dividends, whether that education is formal, in a classroom, or informal, involving family, friends, or community groups. I had come to understand that in a very concrete way, democracy is the collective responsibility of concerned Americans. I wanted to do my part to help.

I've had the good fortune to come to know many of you through our interactions, in person and online. You're strong and compassionate. Whether you live in a red state like me or in a more liberal part of the country, you know we have work to do. In the words of Ben Franklin, a republic, if you can keep it. There is a role ahead for each of us.

I left the private practice of law in 1991 to join the U.S. Attorney's Office in the Northern District of Alabama, thinking it would be just a short career detour. But I learned that there was no higher honor than serving the people of the United States and nothing I wanted to do more. Even after leaving the Justice Department—I resigned the night before Trump's first inauguration in 2017—I felt, and continue to feel, an obligation to share what I had the privilege of learning about our justice system and our democratic institutions during my time in government. But ultimately, it's an educated public capable of informed civil discourse that sustains effective, fair government. Accountability happens when citizens demand it. Sometimes, they must demand it loudly and persistently. This is undoubtedly one of those moments.

Putting these words down on paper makes me feel hopeful. I have always gathered strength from being in community with like-minded people, learning, sharing ideas, and indulging in a little fun and silliness. It's important to resist the conclusion that a move away from democracy is inevitable. It was just this sort of optimism that led me to dash off the words that have become my closing to "Civil Discourse" every night: "We're in this together." That's how I feel about it, even more so now.

It's this belief in our community and in democracy itself that leads me to write to you during such a strange, disturbing moment in American history. A moment when Vice President JD Vance (no relation), a Yale-educated lawyer, suggests that the response to courts that rule against the administration should be ignoring their decisions, when one wonders whether an American president would arrogantly and openly violate an order from a federal judge. Even Richard Nixon turned over the White House tapes when ordered to by the Supreme Court. But by early February 2025, the prospect that President Trump would flout a court order was a very real one. What was I doing writing a book about how to keep the Republic in this moment when, for the first time in my life, I felt the very real possibility that it could be slipping away? It was the only thing I could do.

I spent twenty-five years working at the Justice Department, the only cabinet-level agency whose name is a moral virtue: Justice. I believe in the oath I took, the rule of law, and the way we, as Americans, constantly have to find new ways to work together to make sure more people can experience the promise of America. How can we still believe in our institutions and our rule of law given everything we've experienced in the last decade? I think a better question is, How can we not? What would the alternative look like?

The question is, What can we do to strengthen what has been stretched too thin and reknit the fabric of our democracy so we can fulfill its promise? There's a lot of work ahead of us. We're going to do it together.

CHAPTER I

Don't Be the Frog

There is a well-known, if apocryphal, story about a frog being boiled alive. It goes like this: If you put a frog into a pot of boiling water, it will jump out to save its life because it feels the heat. But if you put that same frog into a pot of room-temperature water and slowly bring it to a boil, the frog won't notice what's happening until it's too late. By the time the danger is upon it, the frog is immobilized and can be cooked until dead.

That metaphor of the frog comes in handy. It is frequently used to illustrate how businesses fail—the warning signs develop so gradually that leadership doesn't shift course until it's too late. It can also describe a troubled romantic relationship that incrementally shades toward abuse. Or societal inaction in the face of climate change. It's also a good, if oversimplified, explanation for how dictators come to power: A slow slide toward tyranny, easily dismissed for far too long by far too much of the populace.

TRUMP AND THE FROGS

We saw this in the United States during the first Trump administration and in the run-up to the 2024 election. It was much easier for some people to pretend we weren't in danger than it was to face the reality that our democracy could come apart. That prospect was far too frightening. They thought, and even today some of them continue to think, that if they don't look, if they unplug from the news or distract themselves with pretty things, it won't happen. The pot gets hotter, but they try to convince themselves that they're still okay.

You might think that having escaped the boiling pot in 2020, when voters put the country back on the path toward democracy, Americans would have been eager to stay out of it. But that wasn't the case. And the speed with which Trump came out of the chute following his 2024 electoral victory, signing more than 140 executive orders that radically altered American democracy during his first hundred days in office, was a jolt of heat.

As they worked through the shock, some Americans finally realized that leaving the pot was their only course of action. They began to assemble and protest. As Trump tried to rewrite the Constitution (birthright citizenship), end legal challenges to his executive orders (attacking law firms), use

DOGE to target federal agencies, disrupt and destroy foreign aid that helped maintain America's relationships and standing in the world, end efforts on climate change, gut universities and colleges, and put a stop to programs that ensured diversity, equity, and inclusion in the federal government, workplaces, and higher education, more people noticed the rising temperature. Bewildered government employees said in interviews that, yes, they had voted for Trump, but they never expected it would cost them *their* jobs.

Part of keeping the Republic is learning, and sometimes relearning, the lesson of the frog. Unfortunately, shock and even horror don't last forever. Some Americans left the pot and then voluntarily jumped back in. Surprise fades away and anger dims. Constant exposure to the heat creates a new normal. Sometimes the frogs fail to learn the lesson and are doomed to repeat their mistakes, until it finally sinks in.

Here is the reality: By the start of the 2024 campaign, the bipartisan outrage that moved some Republicans to criticize Trump after January 6 had dissipated in many parts of the country. Trump made his intention to deconstruct American democracy plain during the 2024 campaign. He continued to claim the 2020 election had been "stolen" from him even though that was a lie. It wasn't much of a stretch to understand he might try to exact revenge on those he believed were involved—he said as much. Despite the clear evidence, many people refused to believe the water would really come to a boil if he was reelected. They'd forgotten what they'd lived through during his first term in office.

In normal times, you would expect outrage from across

the political spectrum over a candidate who repeatedly and mendaciously claimed American elections—but only the ones he lost—were fraudulent, a candidate who demanded officials "find" him enough votes to pull a win out of a loss. A candidate who wanted to overturn the will of American voters should have been untouchable and unelectable, a third-party pariah, even more fringe than a George Wallace or a Lyndon LaRouche. But that doesn't happen when voters act like frogs.

On November 5, 2023, *The Washington Post* ran an article about Trump's plans if he won a second term. It started like this: "Trump and his allies have begun mapping out specific plans for using the federal government to punish critics and opponents should he win a second term, with the former president naming individuals he wants to investigate or prosecute and his associates drafting plans to potentially invoke the Insurrection Act on his first day in office to allow him to deploy the military against civil demonstrations." The right-wing think tank the Heritage Foundation spearheaded Project 2025, with contributions from multiple senior members of Trump's first administration, including cabinet secretaries and a White House chief of staff. It laid out explicit plans for his second administration. And yet, people were surprised when the revenge presidency went full bore. Project 2025 became so unpopular when it was aired in public that Trump took pains to distance himself from it during the campaign. That maneuver largely succeeded. Then, upon his inauguration, Trump's administration started carrying it out—almost to the letter.

Despite the cautionary tale of Trump's first term in office, a lot of frogs managed to ignore the rising temperature. Trump floated the stuff of banana republics, but too many voters focused on the price of eggs. Once he was back in office, implementing a startling array of anti-democratic plans, the surprise was that living through a constitutional crisis had a patina of normalcy to it. It didn't necessarily feel like we were in trouble, especially for people who lacked the interest in or ability to pay close attention to what was transpiring. At dinner or over drinks when I'd raise the news, I experienced reactions like "Don't be a drama queen," or "You're overreacting, it's not as bad as you think it is." That's what was happening if you think back to late January or early February 2025. A lot of people still dismissed the concerns as "just talk." At first, nothing much changed in many people's lives. Maybe a friend or two lost a job. But there was no catastrophic event, nothing like a January 6. Nobody was tearing up the Constitution in the streets. No one was hanged on the Capitol steps. There wasn't a dramatic moment to focus on when democracy was lost. It was easy, or at least easy enough, for the frogs to go on being frogs.

NO KINGS

Our nation's history cautions against dozing off in the face of the kind of danger we were seeing. *The Federalist Papers*, a series of eighty-five essays written between October 1787 and

May 1788 by Alexander Hamilton, John Jay, and James Madison, were published anonymously, under the pen name "Publius." The essays were intended to convince New York delegates to ratify the new Constitution. Today, they offer unique insight into the framers' intent when writing the Constitution and the sort of democracy they hoped to build. In 1788, James Madison titled *Federalist* 51 "The Structure of the Government Must Furnish the Proper Checks and Balances between the Different Departments." Reading Madison's words in 2025 only amplifies how committed Trump seems to be to running straight through the checks and balances and accumulating power in the hands of his own executive branch of government.

Madison understood the practical need for the three branches of government to work together but was wary of placing too much power into a single set of hands. That notion of a separation of powers dated back to a French scholar, judge, and philosopher named Charles-Louis de Secondat, Baron de La Brède et de Montesquieu. We know him as Montesquieu. He developed a theory of government that heavily influenced Madison while he was at work on *The Federalist Papers*. There are echoes of Montesquieu's belief that "government be so constituted as one man need not be afraid of another" in Madison's famous line, "If men were angels, no government would be necessary."

Montesquieu's influential work *The Spirit of the Laws* advocated for what is known as a "trias politica," or separation of powers. Specifically, it proposed dividing government into legislative, executive, and judicial branches, with each branch acting independently, a now familiar structure for a government. If imitation is the sincerest form of flattery, then Madison was Montesquieu's greatest admirer. He wrote in *Federalist* 47, "The accumulation of all powers, legislative, executive, and judiciary, in the same hands, whether of one, a few, or many, and whether hereditary, self-appointed, or elective, may justly be pronounced the very definition of tyranny."

Those words from history might have felt rote, even irrelevant, just a few years ago, too obvious to even a casual observer as to require any reflection. But of course, it is not a few years ago. We are watching what Madison would call "the very definition of tyranny," the effort to consolidate the power of the executive branch—while suppressing Congress, the courts, and the press—in one set of hands, those of an American president. The importance of separating power among three branches of government has never been more apparent. If there is a magic bullet for preserving democracy, it is this: prevent any one branch of government from holding too much power, especially power that the Constitution specifically gives to another branch of government.

Democratic state attorneys general understood this when they joined forces and began heading into court over some of the early executive orders in 2025. The lawsuits, which involved matters including birthright citizenship, federal funding freezes and grant cancellations, DOGE access to information in possession of the Treasury Department, firing federal workers, DOGE's constitutionality, and dramatic reductions of personnel and services at the Department of Education, asked the courts to prevent the president from seizing an outsize share of power for himself. Although the cases involved different substantive issues, their unifying goal was to restrict the president's power to what the Founding Fathers directed in the Constitution. Various plaintiffs, including state attorneys general, civil rights groups, pro-democracy organizations, federal employees, and other individuals harmed by the administration's actions, filed more than one hundred lawsuits in just the first two months that the new administration was in operation. More were filed after that, particularly as Trump's deportation plans heated up. At the heart of these cases was an effort to protect the system envisioned by Montesquieu's trias politica.

The state attorneys general understood the stakes. They went for the source of the heat early, to try to get it under control. A functional judicial branch requires the work of both lawyers and judges. Judges can't just issue rulings on their own. They can't spontaneously hold people in contempt. They need lawyers to get the ball rolling by filing cases. Even then, judges can consider only the issues raised in the lawsuits before them, and only if they have jurisdiction. If a would-be authoritarian wants to put the courts out of business, the first thing they do is "kill all the lawyers," as the bard wrote.

Trump attempted his own version of Shakespeare's infamous line when he launched a series of attacks on prominent law firms, using executive orders and presidential memos, in what looked like little more than an attempt to settle old scores. The first one came in March 2025, targeting a Washington, DC, firm, Covington & Burling, and specifying its supposed wrongdoing—providing Special Counsel Jack Smith, who charged Donald Trump in two criminal cases, with free legal advice. Next he focused on Perkins Coie, where election lawyer Marc Elias worked before going out on his own. The firm's apparent sin was representing Democrats, including in connection with events surrounding the 2016 election. Then he came for more firms, including some of the oldest, most distinguished, and largest firms in the nation: Paul, Weiss; Jenner & Block; Susman Godfrey; and WilmerHale. The orders were separate but similar, with each firm singled out by name. The measures in them, intended to bring the firms to heel, were mob boss–level intimidation, including canceling lawyers' security clearances, denying firm employees access to federal property, terminating existing government contracts the firms had, and characterizing the firms' efforts to be more inclusive as potentially unlawful "racial discrimination."

The first order had come as something of a shock, and that shock was punctuated by each one that followed. These big law firms, perhaps not coincidentally, were well resourced and full of talented lawyers, and they were engaged in at least some work that was adverse to the new administration. Of course, there was the potential for them to bring many more cases as time went on. But the executive orders were harsh enough that some of the firms were concerned about going out of business. Then Paul, Weiss cut a deal with Trump to get out from under the restrictive provisions of his executive order. Others followed, including firms that agreed to Trump's terms before he issued an executive order, to prevent him from publicly naming them. For a moment, it looked like Trump might successfully coerce Big Law to stop bringing the lawsuits challenging the constitutionality of the new administration's policies so that the courts could rule on them. But other firms chose to fight, and as of this writing, they have been universally successful in convincing the lower courts that Trump's actions were unconstitutional, although the cases are not yet over.

When a president speaks in an executive order, the figurative megaphone strapped to his mouth can inflict great damage. The order for WilmerHale started out with the accusation that "many firms take actions that threaten public safety and national security, limit constitutional freedoms, degrade the quality of American elections, or undermine bedrock American principles." Trump then pointed his finger directly at WilmerHale, calling it "yet another law firm that has abandoned the profession's highest ideals and abused its pro bono practice to engage in activities that undermine justice and the interests of the United States." Trump singled out Robert Mueller, the special counsel who investigated him during his first term in office and had once been a partner at WilmerHale. The order stated that "Mueller's 'investigation' upended the lives of public servants in my Administration who were summoned before 'prosecutors' with the effect of interfering in their ability to fulfill the mandates of my first term agenda. This weaponization of the justice system must not be rewarded, let alone condoned." It was clear that these orders weren't about "bedrock American principles." They were tools for revenge. Trump could not let old wounds close, even for the good of the country.

The attacks on the lawyers were not only designed to inflict damage on firms whose clients or partners the president disliked. They were also an attack on the court system itself and on its ability to function as a check against an overly ambitious president as the Founding Fathers had intended. Kneecapping either side of the equation, lawyers or the judges themselves, diminishes the ability of the judiciary to play its role as a check and balance. Attacking both simultaneously made it clear that Trump understood just how important the third branch of government—the courts—was to protecting democracy.

That's the context for the extraordinary—and yet unsurprising—effort early in the second Trump administration to delegitimize the courts. Particularly at the trial court level, judges have shown a willingness and ability to rein in constitutional excesses committed by a runaway president. The Trump administration argued that courts shouldn't second-guess any decisions made by a president, labeling long-established norms of judicial review a "judicial coup." At times, the administration suggested that if it didn't like a court's orders, it could just ignore them. And as Trump's plans for mass deportations of immigrants who were in this country without legal status got bogged down in the courts, there was even a whistleblower complaint. In it, a former DOJ employee alleged that a high-ranking Justice Department official prepared his subordinates to execute the president's plans regardless of any court orders to the contrary that might be entered. The whistleblower claimed that the official, Emil Bove, told subordinates that "DOJ would need to consider telling the courts 'fuck you' and ignore any such court order." The administration and its supporters claimed that if judges persisted in ruling contrary to the president's plans, they should be impeached.

Of course, none of those arguments against judges doing their assigned task of judicial review in the cases before them, no matter how pervasively they were advanced on social media, are consistent with the history and tradition of our system. In fact, the Supreme Court has in recent terms turned to *distant* history and tradition, as in the 2022 decision that stripped American women of the right to obtain an abortion, *Dobbs v. Jackson Women's Health Organization*. Justice Samuel Alito relied on a seventeenth-century English jurist, Sir Matthew Hale, who believed there was no such thing as marital rape and who sentenced women to death for being witches. If that's the standard the Court wants to use, then it should also apply it to the claims that the courts can't review Donald Trump's decisions.

Our history and traditions put the lie to any arguments that the courts can't review an administration's actions for compliance with the Constitution. Trump may want to create a more powerful chief executive, but to the extent he exceeds what the Constitution provides for, it's the courts' job to rein him in, using judicial review. How does that work? To answer that question, let's revisit two canonical court cases, and one failed impeachment, from our nation's past.

First up is a case from the earliest days of the union, and one that all law students encounter in their first few weeks of class: *Marbury v. Madison*. *Marbury* hinged on whether the Supreme Court could declare that a law Congress passed was unconstitutional.

The presidential election of 1800 was between two comrades in arms from the drafting of the Declaration of Independence, the sitting president, John Adams, and his vice president, Thomas Jefferson. They were elected in 1796 after George Washington stepped down. Adams narrowly beat out Jefferson in the Electoral College, which, under the rules of the day, made the winner president and the runner-up vice president. Despite their history together, their rematch in 1800 was an angry campaign with flash points similar to arguments that were raised in 2020 and 2024. Jefferson's Democratic-Republicans disagreed with restrictive policies on citizenship adopted by Adams's Federalists. Accusations flew that the winner intended to become a dictator, as did complaints of interference with free speech. Jefferson emerged, albeit narrowly, as the victor.

The controversy that became *Marbury v. Madison* arose in the waning days of the Adams administration. As the lame-duck president was preparing to hand over power to Jefferson, Congress passed the Judiciary Act of 1801. It created new courts and judgeships, giving Adams last-minute authority to appoint new judges before he left office. Among the new positions were justices of the peace in the District of Columbia, who would be responsible for resolving minor disputes. Adams appointed William Marbury, a prominent businessman, to one of the positions, and he was hurriedly confirmed by the Senate. But despite his commission being properly signed and sealed by the president, Marbury didn't receive it in time. In the chaos of the transition, staff failed to deliver commissions to seventeen new justices of the peace, Marbury among them.

Once in office, Jefferson ordered his secretary of state, James Madison, to withhold delivery of Marbury's commission. Jefferson railed against Adams's "midnight appointments," calling them "an outrage on decency." Adams had provided Jefferson with the ammunition to do so, saying, "I shall secure the future of the judiciary by blocking Mr. Jefferson from making lifetime appointments of judges." Jefferson accused his predecessor of stacking the courts with judges "whose views are to defeat mine." It looked like William Marbury was out of luck.

But Marbury wanted his position, humble as it was, as did some of the other newly appointed justices of the peace. So, they went to court. Marbury wanted the Supreme Court to use its original jurisdiction power to issue a writ of mandamus, an order that would direct Secretary of State Madison to turn over Marbury's commission, as the law required.

Today we mostly think of the Supreme Court as the highest appellate court in our system, but it also has limited original jurisdiction power to hear cases like a trial court does.

This happens in specific circumstances laid out in the Constitution: Cases affecting ambassadors and other public ministers and consuls, and cases where a state is a party. Congress expanded the Court's original jurisdiction in the Judiciary Act of 1789. Marbury's lawyers argued that expanded jurisdiction gave the Court authority to issue the writ of mandamus they requested—authority it did not have under the Constitution.

The chief justice of the day, John Marshall, faced a dilemma. How could he ensure the Supreme Court emerged from the fraught political dispute as an independent branch of government, one that could remain above the fray of the partisan politics of the day? If the Court issued the writ, Madison could just continue to refuse to deliver the commission, and the Court would look weak. If the Court didn't issue it, the judges would appear to have capitulated to the will of the new president. Instead, Marshall found a third path that both resolved the case before the Court and, more importantly, took advantage of its facts to carve out a unique role for the judiciary among the three branches of government. By taking it, Marshall created the power of judicial review, authorizing the Supreme Court to decide whether laws enacted by Congress passed constitutional muster.

Marshall delivered the Court's unanimous opinion from the bench. Poor Marbury didn't get his commission after all because the Court held that even though he was entitled to his judgeship and a writ of mandamus, the Court lacked the jurisdiction to issue the writ.

The Chief Justice concluded that the Judiciary Act of 1789 unconstitutionally expanded the Court's original jurisdiction beyond what the Constitution allowed. Marshall held that the Constitution was the "supreme law of the land" and any law that is inconsistent with it "is void." He explained that it was up to the courts to decide when that was the case. The Supreme Court has the authority to override a law passed by Congress if it conflicts with or violates the Constitution— that's judicial review. "It is emphatically the province and duty of the Judicial Department to say what the law is," and where the Constitution and an ordinary law are in conflict, it is the Constitution that controls. Judicial review positions the Court, arguably the weakest of the three branches of government, to determine when one of the other branches exceeds the scope of its constitutional authority *and* to countermand the unconstitutional act.

Marbury v. Madison establishes the principle of judicial review, which allows courts to assess laws passed by Congress for constitutionality. The contours of judicial review are not laid out in the Constitution, but Chief Justice Marshall understood that if the new nation were to have a functional rule of law, the Supreme Court had to have *both* the authority to deem laws unconstitutional *and* to overrule them so they could not stay in effect in violation of the Constitution.

But what about unconstitutional acts by a president? That part of the equation was explicitly confirmed by the Court in a case heard a century and a half later. By then, plenty of case law already pointed to this obvious conclusion, but the Court made plain: Even a president can't bypass the courts and ignore judges' decisions. In *Youngstown Sheet & Tube Co. v. Sawyer*, decided in 1952, the Supreme Court refused to let President Harry Truman take over US steel mills during the Korean War. Though Truman didn't like the decision, he complied. That's how the rule of law works.

By December 1951, trouble was brewing in the nation's steel mills. There was a dispute with organized labor over wages and working conditions. But the United States had been at war in Korea for more than a year, and China had also entered the fray. Then, negotiations with the United Steelworkers of America, a powerful union, failed. The union filed notice that it would strike at the end of the month when existing agreements with employers expired. Federal mediation with the union was tried and failed. Truman sent the case to the Federal Wage Stabilization Board in an effort to avoid a major disruption of material in such a delicate moment. That failed as well, and the union gave notice that a nationwide strike would commence on April 9, 1952.

The Court explained what President Truman did next in its opinion: "The indispensability of steel as a component of substantially all weapons and other war materials led the President to believe that the proposed work stoppage would immediately jeopardize our national defense and that governmental seizure of the steel mills was necessary in order to assure the continued availability of steel. Reciting these considerations for his action, the President, a few hours before the strike was to begin, issued Executive Order 10340. . . . The order directed the Secretary of Commerce to take possession of most of the steel mills and keep them running." The issue before the Court was whether a president had the power to take this action via executive order.

The steel companies tried to fight off the executive order in court, arguing that the president lacked the power to make the seizures because neither the Constitution nor an act of Congress granted it to him. On April 30, 1952, the district court ruled in their favor and enjoined the government's seizure. The court of appeals weighed in the same day, but it came to the opposite conclusion. It stayed the district court's injunction, which meant the president could move forward. In a display of the speed with which the Supreme Court can act when motivated, it granted certiorari, agreeing to hear the case on May 3, and set it for oral argument on May 12.

Plenty of case law from the intervening 149 years since *Marbury* pointed toward the conclusion the Supreme Court reached in *Youngstown*, but its decision settled the matter once and for all. The Court explained that since there was no law passed by Congress granting the president the authority to seize the steel mills, the only place that power could come from was the Constitution. President Truman didn't claim (nor could he have) that the power was specifically found in the Constitution. Rather, his solicitor general argued that it was implied, considering all the powers given to the president in that document, especially Article II of the Constitution, which provides that "the executive Power shall be vested in a President"; that "he shall take Care that the Laws be faithfully executed"; and that he "shall be Commander in Chief of the Army and Navy of the United States."

The Supreme Court didn't bite at this early expression of what would become known as the unitary executive theory. It rejected the suggestion that the president could make laws, writing that he could suggest ones "he thinks wise" and veto ones "he thinks bad" and no more. The power to create laws, the Court reiterated, belongs to Congress, and to Congress exclusively. The Court concluded that Truman's seizures were unconstitutional, explaining that "the President's order does not direct that a congressional policy be executed in a manner prescribed by Congress—it directs that a presidential policy be executed in a manner prescribed by the President." The Court held that while Congress could have adopted laws that would make this kind of action lawful, it had not, and that the "Constitution does not subject this lawmaking power of Congress to presidential or military supervision or control."

WITH THE PRINCIPLE FIRMLY ESTABLISHED THAT THE SUPREME Court can tell a president no when his actions exceed the scope of his constitutional power, our final lesson comes not from a court case but from an impeachment: that of Justice Samuel Chase in 1804, a year after *Marbury v. Madison* was decided. The Constitution sets forth some limits regarding the service of federal judges. Article III provides that they are to remain on the bench as long as they engage in "good Behavior" and that their salary cannot be reduced while in office. But Article I includes judges among the cohort of civil officers who can be impeached by the House for "high Crimes and

Misdemeanors" and removed from office if the Senate convicts them on those charges. That ambiguous phrase, "high Crimes and Misdemeanors," means more than just crimes that are on the books, but how far it extends is unclear. Constitutional law scholars Laurence Tribe and Joshua Matz wrote in their 2018 book, *To End a Presidency*, that the designation includes grave abuses of power and betrayals of the public trust, "intentional, evil deeds" that "drastically subvert the Constitution and involve an unforgivable abuse of the presidency"—even if they fall short of a technical violation of the law. Judges could be removed for criminal and other serious misconduct. But could they be impeached for their legal decisions if someone with political power objected to them?

We are back to Thomas Jefferson's presidency. Jefferson wanted the House of Representatives to impeach Chief Justice Chase, and it most definitely had to do with the politics of the day. The official Senate account of the proceedings refers to Chase as "a staunch Federalist with a volcanic personality." One of Chase's duties as a judge was to charge new grand juries, organizing them for their term of service and explaining the procedure to them. Jefferson, the leader of the Democratic-Republican Party, became angry when he learned that Chase had charged a grand jury in a way Jefferson believed had an unfair political slant. He wrote to the House and asked them to impeach.

The articles of impeachment charged Chase with acting in a political manner during the grand jury proceedings. The articles also addressed rulings he made in other cases involving treason and sedition, including refusing to dismiss allegedly biased grand jurors and excluding or limiting defense witnesses in politically sensitive cases. It was, as we have previously noted, still an acrimonious and unsettled time in the formation of the new nation. It would have been easy for America's young democracy to have gone off the rails here.

The House impeached Chase, but as we know from our modern-day experience, articles of impeachment, like an indictment, are merely charges brought against someone accused of misconduct. That person is still entitled to a trial, and in Chase's case, the Senate did not vote to convict, even though Jefferson's Democratic-Republican Party held a supermajority and the Senate was presided over by Jefferson's vice president, Aaron Burr, who, as Chief Justice William Rehnquist noted in a piece on the tumultuous events, was "a fugitive from justice at the time, having killed Alexander Hamilton in a duel at Weehawken, New Jersey, the preceding summer." It almost makes politics in 2025 look tame.

The failed impeachment stood for an important proposition. Rehnquist put it like this: The fact that a political heavyweight doesn't like a judge's decision should not be a basis for removing judges from the bench. We have learned that the Constitution requires judges to decide what the law *is*. It stands to reason that they should not be impeached for doing that job. Judges do get impeached from time to time. But those situations almost always involve outright criminal behavior, not a complaint from someone who doesn't like the way they ruled in a particular case. That's the point of having an independent judiciary. It maintains its independence from political forces that seek to influence it for their own advantage, so it can preserve the level playing field that allows our politics to play out as constitutionally intended, at the will of the people.

Any would-be autocrat has to consider how to avoid, even derail, judicial review. An independent branch of government that can block their authoritarian efforts to seize more and more power is a threat to their chance of success. Indeed, judicial review is one of our most essential aids in challenging times, so long as judges live up to the role assigned to them. For the rest of us, people who have had the good fortune to live in a country where we were able to take the continued existence of democracy for granted for so many years, understanding how this works is no longer optional. Understanding how government works and how it is supposed to work is essential to resisting those who would fuel the fire that boils the water that kills the frogs.

The Supreme Court Historical Society concluded its assessment of *Marbury v. Madison* like this: "Although President Jefferson complained about the 'twistifications' in Marshall's logic, the Democratic-Republicans accepted the *Marbury v. Madison* decision. This was because Marshall had chosen to assert judicial review with a case that recognized the power of Congress and limited the Court's power. The Supreme Court has since relied on the Marbury precedent to ensure that government acts comply with the Constitution in a variety of pivotal cases affecting the political, economic and social fabric of the nation." That assessment perhaps understates the force of *Marbury*, which has withstood the test of time for almost 225 years, ensuring that Congress has the power to make laws, and the president the power to enforce and implement them. But it is up to the courts to decide what is and what isn't constitutional. They have kept the system in balance, allowing the frogs to sleep in the pot complacently for decades. If a president no longer has to worry that judicial review will restrain wild excesses of power, then the pot will come to a boil, and fast.

ATTACKING OTHER BRANCHES
OF GOVERNMENT

The way our system works and should work is clear. But a powerful campaign to change the rules was already under-way early in the second Trump administration. In normal times, a naked effort to delegitimize the judiciary would have been rejected by outraged bipartisan alliances of lawyers in Congress, government, and private practice. But these aren't normal times. The ability of judges and lawyers to fulfill their roles is under threat from the new administration. As Supreme Court Justice Ketanji Brown Jackson put it in a talk at a conference of judges and lawyers in May 2025, "The attacks are not random. They seem designed to intimidate those of us who serve in this critical capacity. The threats and ha-rassment are attacks on our democracy, on our system of government. And they ultimately risk undermining our Con-stitution and the rule of law." She received a standing ovation from the attendees at the end of her talk, in which she called on the judges in the room to show "raw courage" and dis-pense justice without fear of any outside consequences. "I urge you to keep going, keep doing what is right for our country, and I do believe that history will vindicate your service." History and, if we get this right, the American people.

The efforts to undermine the judiciary suggest dark days ahead. That's why the Shakespeare quote about killing all the lawyers continues to resonate. No lawyers, no pesky rule of law to worry about. Dictators like to cloak their early steps in the appearance of legality. That's easier to do when there are no lawyers around and no courts to rule against them.

AT THIS LATE DATE, THERE IS NO LONGER ANY EXCUSE FOR BEING A frog. The temperature of the water is undeniable. There is no reason for a head of government to undermine the judicial branch unless they fear its ability to hold them accountable. Our understanding of the importance of living in a rule of law country got a refresh when "due process" became a rallying cry for Americans who protested in outrage over the administration's unconstitutional deportation practices. Although it was difficult, even for lawyers, to follow all the details in the deluge of litigation challenging the Trump administration, it was clear that the new president was trying to aggregate the power of the three branches of government in his own hands.

Attacks like these are openers. They may start with relatively modest encroachments, but once the ability of the judiciary to stand as a check has been undermined, there are no limits. The German pastor Martin Niemöller understood that, having lived through Hitler's Germany. He wrote these words in 1946, reflecting:

> First they came for the socialists, and I did not speak out—because I was not a socialist.
> Then they came for the trade unionists, and I did not speak out—because I was not a trade unionist.
> Then they came for the Jews, and I did not speak out—because I was not a Jew.
> Then they came for me—and there was no one left to speak for me.

The frogs refuse to see the larger picture. If they come for the judges, they are not coming for just the judges. They will come for the law firms, one at a time. They will, and they did, come for federal employees, transgender people, immigrants, universities, librarians, the press, epidemiologists, scientists, and others.

People can succumb to fear when faced with the bully, the authoritarian. America has often worked best when coalitions have formed to prevent anyone from being singled out, ostracized, and marginalized. The time-honored tradition of Americans is to stand together.

In *Federalist* 51, James Madison aptly characterized justice as the goal of having a government in the first place: "Justice is the end of government. It is the end of civil society. It ever has been and ever will be pursued until it be obtained, or until liberty be lost in the pursuit." When it comes to eroding a democracy and taking away people's rights and freedom, the people doing the taking are counting on the frogs' willingness to endure and ignore the slow application of heat. The answer is to jump out of the pot before it comes to a boil, and bring the other frogs with you as well.

CHAPTER 2

The Myth of Broken Institutions

I n the popular imagination, Donald Trump is invincible. But that's a myth, not reality. Every would-be authoritarian in history has tried to assume the mantle of inevitability. But here's an essential, often overlooked truth about the United States: In significant ways, both big and small, it has subtle advantages when it comes to retaining democracy, chief among them our institutions. Even under stress, they can be nimble. They can take on new challenges, just the way they did during and after the Civil War, through two world wars, during the Depression, in the aftermath of Watergate, and following 9/11. They evolve; they have reach. These institutions are populated by individuals with a deep commitment to democracy, the career civil service. And beyond them there are civil society groups, the military, lawyers, unions, students, and teachers, each with their own commitments to ensuring the continuation of democracy. Our voting infrastructure is decentralized—we hold fifty state elections, not one federal one—so no one person can take control of it. Those state elections are usually run at the county level by everyday Americans.

We are a democracy with almost 250 years of history behind us. We have democracy at the federal level, but also at the state and local levels. We order our society in a democratic fashion so deeply ingrained that although we have fallen into the habit of taking it for granted, it is the foundation for our way of life.

Institutions have carried our democracy this far. They can take us forward in the face of this newest challenge. They have not been irredeemably broken, as some would have us believe. These institutional naysayers are at best frightened and at worst have something to gain if our institutions grow weak and people give up on them.

AS JOE BIDEN'S TERM AS PRESIDENT CAME TO A CLOSE IN JANUARY 2025, Donald Trump had, for the most part, outrun the criminal justice system. The two federal prosecutions against him foundered, not for lack of merit but because of delays interposed by his legal team. Trump floated a narrative that took hold with his voters: that the thirty-four felony counts he was convicted of in a New York state courtroom were minor, and that he was the true victim. By the time he won the 2024 election, some Americans felt that not only had Trump broken the law but also that he had broken the *rule of law*; that our institutions were so irrevocably flawed that we should abandon them.

That sort of defeatism is not who we are. Democrats may have lost the last election, but that's not the same thing as losing the Republic. Far from it. And Donald Trump did not break the rule of law. He may have tortured it and stretched it out of shape as applied to him, but he has not broken it, and he has not broken us. He cannot do that unless we let him. In 2025, Americans who believe in democracy picked themselves back up and began to fight again.

THE RULE OF LAW AND OUR INSTITUTIONS

Whether we knew it at the start of Trump's time in office, what we were fighting for was the rule of law. "The rule of law" is one of those phrases that roll off of lawyers' tongues— you hear it in the media, but people rarely stop to define it. In shorthand, one way to think about it is as the principle that no man is above the law; that we have no kings. That's a good starting point. Although the rule of law entails more than that, this core concept lays bare why a would-be authoritarian must first disassemble the rule of law. As long as it's in place, it acts as a barrier against the installation of a strongman with absolute power. The rule of law, in other words, is our essential protection and the last resort to keep at bay someone who wants to seize control.

We saw the rule of law in action in 2025, as soon as Trump began issuing unconstitutional executive orders. Instead of violence in the streets, we had lawyers in courtrooms, challenging the legality of actions by the executive branch. They asked courts for, and frequently received, temporary and preliminary injunctions, legal devices that freeze the status quo, preventing new policies from going into effect until the courts can sort them out. As long as that rule of law process continues to work, we have a powerful tool for protecting democracy.

How does the aspiring dictator fight back? By attacking the fundamentals of the rule of law itself. Trump claimed it was acceptable for a president to ignore court decisions that went against him. Obedience to court orders is ingrained deeply enough in our system that at least in the early months of his administration, Trump set off alarm bells—at times even among members of his own party—when he hinted at an outright refusal to comply with a court's decision. In April 2025, the case of a Salvadoran man, Kilmar Armando Abrego Garcia, came to the Supreme Court after the government deported him despite the existence of an order prohibiting them from doing that because he had a credible fear he would face serious persecution. It was an "administrative error," the government told the Court. The Supreme Court did not go as far as it could have; there was no inquiry into whether the administration intentionally violated the order. But a unanimous Supreme Court—something we don't see too often these days—ordered the Trump administration to "facilitate" Abrego Garcia's return from Salvadoran custody to the United

States. Ultimately, it falls to the courts to stand for the rule of law when it is under attack. They must do so if it's to hold.

The administration's other strategy for setting aside the rule of law was delegitimizing judges who ruled against its new policies. The speed with which federal judges appointed by Trump during his first term were recast as liberals was nothing short of astonishing. All of it was part of a deliberate effort to blunt the effectiveness of the rule of law.

In hindsight it's easy to see the lesson—don't inflict damage on the essential institutions. The would-be autocrat will do that himself. When the public perpetuates narratives that the institutions are broken and talks about walking away from them, it plays into his hands and makes his ascension to power that much easier. The path to autocracy is littered with battered and broken institutions. If you want to preserve democracy, fight for the institutions. Our institutions are not perfect. It's important to acknowledge their problems and commit to improving them, but not abandon the institutions altogether. Criticize the people who are doing the damage to them, the people who seek to destroy democracy, but don't fault the institutions for the flaws of their attackers. Protect the institutions themselves.

That's something we can all do. In our daily conversations. With the way we vote. It starts with how we permit the public discourse to be framed. Take federal employees—the bureaucracy. If they are widely demonized and become generally viewed as do-nothings who waste federal money, or as political enemies of the leader, it's easy for a would-be authoritarian to get people to accept the idea of firing them, and then replacing them with his own loyal troops. That's how a strong institution that protects democracy gets taken apart. Narratives become powerful over time, and they can be dehumanizing. They can also turn institutions that are essential to our well-being into the enemy. Fight back.

THE POWERS OF THE AMERICAN PRESIDENCY ARE BEST UNDER-stood in the context of the rights of kings. Or rather, in contrast to them, because that's the situation the Founding Fathers were trying to avoid. Kings can declare war and deploy forces; they have all the power. In our Constitution, the president is the general in charge of the military, but his power is shared and constrained. Only Congress can declare war.

The Federalist Papers explain the architecture of our government, particularly the division of power. Presidents are elected to terms of four years, and are limited, with an assist from the Twenty-Second Amendment, to serving no more than two terms. They can be impeached for misconduct and, in the language of *Federalist* 69, "afterwards be liable to prosecution and punishment in the ordinary course of law." In other words, a president is not supposed to be a king. That is central to the balance of power established by the Founding Fathers, who sought to guard against the concentration of power in one place.

At this point, we need to return to the unitary executive theory. It's a theory about presidential power that originated on the far right of the political spectrum among proponents who desired a powerful, even an omnipotent, presidency.

Now it's in vogue. In fact, to its Trumpian proponents, it's the only theory about the presidency that matters.

The unitary executive theory came from small-government conservatives who were concerned that an expansive sprawl of executive branch agencies seemed destined to wrest the lawful powers of a president out of his grasp at the same time both the courts and Congress were shackling the president's power. They believed that post-Watergate reforms had gone too far. The unitarians reasoned that because Article II, Section 1 of the Constitution provides that "the executive Power shall be vested in a President of the United States of America," the president must hold all, or at least most, of that power, to wield as he pleases, unimpeded by the courts, Congress, or civil servants in the federal bureaucracy. Harvard Law professors Cass R. Sunstein and Adrian Vermeule argue that when interpreting Section 1 of Article II, "Those words do not seem ambiguous. Under the Constitution, the President, and no one else, has executive power." It's an extreme, muscular vision of the presidency.

Strikingly, the current version of the unitary executive seems to turn the sensibilities of small-government conservatives on their head. It would permit a president to make all decisions while demanding unquestioning allegiance from the executive branch workforce. Anything else, so the explanation goes, would prevent the president from fully implementing whatever mandate he believes the voters have given him. Rather than doing away with the conservatives' hated nanny state, today's unitary executive seems to want to control it for himself. In its most extreme expressions, the unitary executive cannot be prosecuted for criminal acts committed in office as long as they are arguably connected to official duties. That's how the Supreme Court saw it in *Trump v. United States* in 2024. This unitary executive can swamp the other two branches of government, behaving in ways no other citizen or institution can. In practice, it's less a political theory and more a power grab.

You do not need to make a detailed study of the legal doctrine to understand that adopting it as a theory of how the presidency should operate has major real-world consequences. The view is consonant with how autocrats have operated in other backsliding democracies, such as Hungary, where Viktor Orbán took tightfisted control of executive powers in a fashion described in a policy brief from the European Council on Foreign Relations as "the key to being able to eventually establish control over the broader institutions of governance and civil society."

Just ask the recipients of programs administered by US-AID who found them suddenly ripped away. The malnourished children who required the food that was left to rot on shelves. Or the older people who required oxygen and other medical assistance to stay alive but did not get it. Ask the career federal employees who lost their jobs and, instead of being thanked for their public service, suffered the additional insult of being labeled unnecessary waste by DOGE. As National Public Radio's Scott Detrow explained in an interview on *All Things Considered*, "The choice to unilaterally dissolve a federal agency, one established by Congress, was a shock to Washington. But the concept at the heart of it—that the president has broad authority to act unilaterally without consequence, that the executive branch should reflect his priorities—stems from one idea, the unitary executive theory." Donald Trump took it and ran with it.

Make no mistake: The Founding Fathers *did* believe in a powerful executive. But they emphasized, at the same time, that a president must be accountable. *The Federalist Papers* may seem to some to be the stuff of dry history. It's time to change that. There is a lot they can teach us that matters today if we're going to hold on to democracy.

The Founding Fathers expected the courts and Congress to act as a check on the presidency, not to succumb to it. Consider the power of the president to make foreign treaties and agreements. The founders concluded that power should be shared with the Senate. In *Federalist* 75, Hamilton wrote:

> It must indeed be clear to a demonstration that the joint possession of the power in question, by the President and Senate, would afford a greater prospect of security, than the separate possession of it by either of them.

There was real appetite at the time of the founding to carefully allocate power and impose checks and balances because the colonists were done with the rule of kings. That plays out differently today, especially when the same party controls the White House and one or both bodies in Congress.

There was that standout country-over-party moment during Watergate when Nixon's criminal conduct had been exposed and Senate Republicans turned their backs on him. But that approach is not the rule. These days, a Senate majority aligned with a president will confirm almost anyone a president puts up for confirmation. When the Senate majority belongs to the opposition, even excellent nominees are rejected.

Our institutions have constitutional strengths that help them act as leveling agents against a seizure of power by any one among them. When a branch abandons some of its prerogatives, the resulting imbalance emphasizes the importance of ensuring each branch fulfills its constitutionally assigned role. It helps us understand the importance of having a civil service loyal to the Constitution and its mission, not to any one president. It underscores why due diligence is required of the Senate before it votes to confirm nominees (lest we get a cabinet secretary who believes habeas corpus is a president's right to remove people from the country, not the right those people have to challenge unconstitutional confinement). Frustration with institutions that don't perform effectively is legitimate, but it's critical to get the diagnosis right. Often it's the people who populate them who are flawed, not the institutional framework itself.

Human beings are attracted to power, and even the best-intentioned people can find the temptation hard to resist. When that power is the power of government, power over the people, it must be protected zealously from abuse. In *Federalist* 51, Madison wrote about the potential problems in terms that ring true today: "It may be a reflection on human nature, that such devices should be necessary to control the abuses of government. But what is government itself but the greatest of all reflections on human nature?"

Madison understood that elected officials, and especially presidents, would not always prioritize our "communal interests," that government officials would inevitably push legislation and policies that were in their own interests, not their constituents'. And so the Founding Fathers created a system designed to protect people from government, one entrenched in the institutions themselves. In order to keep the presidency from becoming too powerful, Congress and the courts hold some share of power for their own and have the ability to check the executive branch. Other institutions, like the press, the unofficial fourth branch of government, hold a president accountable by educating the electorate. Our military is civilian led, a deliberate choice made to lessen the risk of a military coup. And in the post-Watergate era, at least until recently, the Justice Department has not taken orders from the White House when deciding who should be prosecuted and who shouldn't be. Instead, it has made those decisions independently, based solely on the facts and the law, so criminal prosecution cannot be wielded as a political tool.

It is the balance among the institutions, as much as the institutions themselves, that provides security for our democracy. As noted, it has become, in recent decades, popular to bash institutions—and let's be clear, they bring much of that upon themselves. They could do better; in some cases, far better. But our goal must be to strengthen them so they can function fully on our behalf, especially at a time when we are led by people who are comfortable damaging them to further their own interests over societal ones. We must stand for the institutions and insist on their health and their performance, which we can often advance with our votes and even more so with our voices.

And so, when Hamilton wrote in *Federalist* 73 about Congress's ability to override a presidential veto of newly enacted legislation, he did so with precision, explaining why a presidency in danger of running amok might need to be held in check by Congress: "When men, engaged in unjustifiable pursuits, are aware that obstructions may come from a quarter which they cannot control, they will often be restrained by the bare apprehension of opposition, from doing what they would with eagerness rush into, if no such external impediments were to be feared." The mere perception that a check is securely in place can be enough to constrain presidential overreach, as when Donald Trump considered but refrained from firing special counsel Robert Mueller while Mueller was investigating him.

WHY THE INSTITUTIONS MATTER

A president who wants to do away with restraints on the way he exercises power will weaken, or try to fatally damage, the institutions that can check him. Some people believe Donald Trump has already done that. That view—like the one that sees Trump's ascendancy as inevitable—fails to recognize the resilience built into our institutions. Even when they've been battered, they can still find ways to fulfill their constitutional obligation to act as a check, which is especially important in a moment when the unitary executive philosophy has been paired with a president willing to push it.

That takes us back to the judiciary. In *Federalist* 78, Hamilton wrote that "the judiciary is beyond comparison the weakest of the three departments of power; that it can never attack with success either of the other two; and that all possible care is requisite to enable it to defend itself against their attacks." The courts must defend themselves from being hollowed out and placed in a position of inferiority to the other branches of government.

A recent example demonstrates this point. In *Trump v. United States*, the case that gave a president broad immunity from prosecution for his official acts, the Supreme Court allowed the executive branch to renegotiate the terms of the balance of power among the three branches of government in its favor. They forgot the lesson Hamilton taught, that fear of consequences can prevent an abuse of power. They also removed, in service of the unitary executive theory, virtually all the risk of prosecution for crimes committed by a president while in office. Justice Neil Gorsuch said during oral argument that the Court was "writing a rule for the ages." He would have done better to concern himself with the present and with maintaining the balance of power the founders set so carefully.

The courts must be ever mindful, as Hamilton says, to protect their own institution from attack. When they fail to do so, they upset the three-legged stool that our government must rest upon if it is to stay in balance. The much-repeated canard about President Andrew Jackson dismissing a Supreme Court ruling against him, saying, "John Marshall has made his decision, now let him enforce it," turns out to have likely been more legend than history. But it is a reminder of the delicate position the judiciary is in. It also explains why judges give litigants before them every opportunity to self-correct before they take steps to sanction them. It is not weakness that compels them to do this, but a forthright understanding of the power and the limits of the institution they serve in.

Despite this, the judiciary is not defenseless. It has powers it can deploy to maintain its strength as an institution and perform its important checks-and-balances function—if it chooses to use them. Courts have both civil and criminal contempt powers, and although there is great concern about the prospect of the executive branch flouting a court order and refusing to submit to sanctions for contempt, the political cost of such an outright violation of constitutional order, if it came to that, could prove to be an administration's undoing.

Much has been written about the public's loss of confidence in the courts—or to be more precise, the Supreme Court. The Court has retreated from long-standing precedent—including, most infamously, *Roe v. Wade*, despite many of the justices testifying in their confirmation hearings that it was unassailable. The Court has faced highly public ethics scandals, and not being bound by an ethics code like the rest of the judiciary, they have declined to act internally and hold Justices Samuel Alito and Clarence Thomas accountable for accepting expensive gifts from people who have an interest in outcomes of cases before the Court and engaging in behavior that could cause a reasonable person to question their impartiality. As a result, the Supreme Court now commands one of its lowest approval ratings in the time that data has been collected. One roundup of polls characterized the Court's position as "in the gutter." In September 2023, Gallup concluded it was near an all-time low. But again, it is not the structural institution itself that is lacking; it is the people who populate it and their personal failures. Our job as citizens is not to abandon the courts but rather to demand better from them.

Ideally, the Court would take the lead in sustaining its own integrity. When problems occur, and they inevitably will, it should address them transparently in order to maintain public confidence—no one is above the law. Perception has a way of becoming reality, and no institution, let alone one this important, can afford to appear as though it's teetering. The courts, lacking an army to enforce their decisions, are able to function because the public has confidence in them as neutral arbiters and is willing to accept decisions they disagree with because they believe the process is fair. Without public confidence, the courts would be a toothless tiger.

But that is not where we are. Our courts continue to function, ruling on thousands of matters before them every year. Every day, trial judges patiently explain the process to juries. Courts of appeals write decisions that can frequently be understood, even if not agreed with, by everyone. The Supreme Court is not the entirety of the court system. Indeed, some district judges and court of appeals judges seem to have grasped the credibility issue more readily than the Supreme Court has. But the public's confidence in the high court is essential and the justices must do more to protect it. The Supreme Court may well end up being the pivotal institution that has the last, best chance to prevent an elected president from transforming into a full-blown autocrat.

The courts are capable of functioning as a mature democratic institution, like they did in the wake of the 2020 election when judges appointed by Republican and Democratic presidents alike ruled that the presidential election was not tainted by fraud and ensured there would be a smooth transfer of power from one administration to the next. The courts preserved our fragile democracy in that moment. We should not abandon them now. Ultimately, and notwithstanding concerns about the willingness of some judges to let politics and personalities intrude on their mission, courts are the institution with power to stand against a president who would overreach.

The courts' greatest strength is the power of judicial review, which we have discussed previously. They can exercise it over laws passed by Congress and orders given and actions taken by presidents to prevent those branches of government from straying from the constraints imposed by the Constitution. Alexander Hamilton explained the importance of judicial review in *Federalist* 78. "There is no position which depends on clearer principles, than that every act of a delegated authority, contrary to the tenor of the commission under which it is exercised, is void," Hamilton wrote. The courts decide what the Constitution means.

Hamilton wrote *Federalist* 78 and expounded on the rationale for judicial review fifteen years before the Supreme Court formalized it in *Marbury v. Madison.* But even when he was writing, the key point was clear: The font of our laws is the Constitution, and neither legislature nor executive can go beyond or outside it. Hamilton wrote, "No legislative act, therefore, contrary to the Constitution, can be valid. To deny this, would be to affirm, that the deputy is greater than his principal; that the servant is above his master; that the representatives of the people are superior to the people themselves; that men acting by virtue of powers may do not only what their powers do not authorize, but what they forbid." The same reasoning applies to prevent an imperial presidency.

If we stand back and take in the big picture of an institution like the courts, we can see its solidity even if the people who currently populate it have flaws. This is true not just for the courts but for all of our democratic institutions. We can criticize them when they come up short, while still understanding that they have the enduring strength that makes us capable of outlasting attacks on our democracy.

WHERE DO WE FIT IN?

Believing in the institutions means that we must also believe in ourselves. Their power is our power. Collectively, as voters, as citizens, as concerned Americans, we have power. We are as essential a democratic institution as the three branches of government. As voters, we direct the priorities our elected officials must focus on if they want to remain in office. A quick example illustrates this. When voters want politicians to be "tough on crime," policies that focus on rehabilitating people are less likely to be adopted. But when the public demands "smart on crime" policies based on statistics that show community-centered support programs are the best way to reduce recidivism, elected officials will vote for them. Voters frame the conversation and set the direction of policy, especially when they use their voices effectively.

The challenge comes in exercising that power. We still, as I'm writing to you, have a First Amendment right to assemble and to petition our government, a right to free speech and a free press. They are ours to insist upon or lose. Americans must insist.

We have a right to vote. We must prepare for the upcoming midterm elections. Despite concerns Trump will try to keep them from happening, that would provoke so much outrage that it is far more likely he will take the easier path, the one that is already set—trying to suppress the votes of people Republicans believe will not vote for them. We'll talk about exercising this right in more detail in chapter 5, but here's an important takeaway to start with. In the 2024 election, 64.1 percent of eligible Americans voted. While that is the second-highest level of turnout in the last century, it still means that roughly one-third of Americans didn't vote. How many of them regret that decision now?

Lawyers talk about "the practice" of law. We are "practicing" because we are constantly learning more, developing our skills, and getting better at it. We learn from our mistakes. We work harder. We get it right. We continue to practice. As Americans, we should treat democracy the same way: the *practice* of democracy, something we do together as Americans. When we make mistakes, even big ones, we can learn from them. We dig deeper so we can fix them. We get back to work. But what we cannot do is give up.

Don't give up on the institutions. We need them. The one thing that's certain is that if we just shrug our shoulders, kleptocracy, corruption, and autocracy will find fertile soil to grow in. Don't just throw up your hands in the air and accept the demise of democracy. We are still a rule of law country. Insist on it. Practice democracy. History teaches us that progress is not linear and that people who want to have a democracy, who understand that it's worth fighting for, must stay the course even at their lowest point. We have two choices: give up or move forward. It's not even close. We have a republic to keep, and we are not quitters.

CHAPTER 3

How Democracy Works for Us

A malaise gripped parts of the country, especially among Democrats, after the 2024 election: Many Americans were ready to give up on democracy. Some were exhausted by the campaign and deeply disturbed by the outcome of the election, devastated to have lost after putting so much into the race. Others, especially some younger voters, weren't as attached to the idea of democracy as earlier generations were. It's easier to walk away when you have no memory of living in a functional democracy, when the first presidency you experienced was Trump's first term. People on social media said they were done. They had given their all and it wasn't working. Why not just burn it all down?

Many of the complaints in this vein dissipated once Trump took office and the threat of actually losing democracy suddenly seemed quite real. But it's concerning that some people were ready to give up, even if only temporarily. It begs the question that is at the very core of this book: Why is democracy, despite its imperfections, worth having?

The extreme end point of the "burn it all down" argument is such severe disillusionment that the questioner ends up thinking: *The system never worked. Why should we work to save it?* Here's an answer: If we acknowledge that American democracy was marred by its flaws at birth—slavery, misogyny, and classism among them—we must also acknowledge that it is capable of advancing beyond them and continuously expanding the groups of people and individuals to whom it extends its promise. That progress may not always be linear. It may not always stick at first. But we have a trajectory that shows that progress is possible, and democracy is at its best when and because citizens demand it. Is progress easy? Has it ever been? Of course not. But when faced with the possibility of losing democracy in early 2025, Americans took to the streets. We understood the cost of losing it.

DEMOCRACY IS, BY ITS NATURE, ASPIRATIONAL. THERE IS ALWAYS more that we can and should do, always a challenge that's imperative to tackle next. We must keep reaching. But fixating exclusively on what remains to be done mars our understanding of what we've accomplished and, more importantly, of what we can accomplish in the future. Despite its inherent imperfections, our democracy has advanced equality, freedom, and justice.

I'm not suggesting that we should ignore the problems. Our prisons need reform; our infrastructure is aging. Too many people go without the medical care they need or have to work more than one job just to make ends meet. And on top of those substantive issues, add the fact that we are living in a moment of grotesque anti-democratic backsliding that is harming both people and institutions at an astonishing rate. It will require years of hard work to fix the problems and restore the institutions. But if we care about those issues, democracy gives us the best chance of finding a fix.

In the spring of 2025, we got to see firsthand what happens when a political party forgets it's supposed to serve the people, not itself. Republican Senator Joni Ernst of Iowa was taking questions at a town hall meeting when she was asked about proposed changes to Medicaid that would drastically reduce coverage for low-income Americans. While she was answering, someone in the crowd called out, "People are going to die." Ernst responded flippantly that "We all are going to die." During the ensuing uproar, Ernst issued the most sarcastic of non-apologies. In a video filmed in a cemetery, she drawled, "I made an incorrect assumption that everyone in the auditorium understood that, yes, we are all going to perish from this earth. So, I apologize and I'm really, really glad that I did not have to bring up the subject of the Tooth Fairy as well." Then she encouraged people who wanted eternal life to "embrace my lord and savior, Jesus Christ."

The senator needs a reminder of who she works for. Despite the challenges, American democracy is *ours*, quite literally the people's. We have the ability to shape and reshape the ongoing American experiment within the system the Founding Fathers created in a way that other governments—theocracies, dictatorships, monarchies—don't offer. One major point of the exercise: We don't have kings. When our representatives fail us, we can replace them. Our history confirms that over the sweep of time, we the people can make significant, incredible, sometimes even glorious progress.

So, how could a shortsighted notion like "Forget about voting, let's burn it all down" gain any currency? Once the trappings of slick TikTok videos have been peeled back, what it really amounts to is *Let's ignore what's happening so a dictator can take over.* One need only look at former Soviet satellite states that were so eager to turn away from communism and toward democracy, or the surge of the Arab Spring, to see that people who live under monarchies or dictatorships desperately long for what we have, even if it's imperfect. They'd prefer to determine the course of their own lives rather than let a leader who *took* power do it for them. As the canny Winston Churchill noted, "It has been said that democracy is the worst form of Government except for all those other forms that have been tried from time to time."

Understanding American democracy means accepting that it will always be aspirational. There will always be more that we should do. In "normal" times, that means pushing to expand the promise of democracy to more people. Progress means we discover additional areas where the veneer of democracy is too thin. It's the story of the waves of immigration to America and how, as groups who had been excluded from the full promise of citizenship fought for inclusion and became more accepted, the next wave of immigrants had to fight that same fight for themselves. It is the story of immigrants from places like Ireland and Italy, the story of European Jews, of Latin American, Indian, Chinese, and Vietnamese immigrants, and many others. Race, religion, national origin, gender, sexual orientation, disabilities—despite the ongoing struggle over all of these, our trajectory has been toward becoming a more diverse America, with more people included in the melting pot. The *other* can become *us*, sometimes with amazing rapidity, as it did in this century, when same-sex marriage went from being forbidden by law to being widely accepted. There is always the promise that we can do better in the future.

But in more challenging times, like the ones we currently face, we get a direct whiff of just how important our democracy is. It's far easier for people in a democracy, even one with some tarnish on it, to redirect the course a country takes than it is for people, say, in a country with an authoritarian government or one reemerging from communism. American democracy comes with some important built-ins: the ability of citizens to vote and elect representatives at all levels of government and the protections of the rule of law, including due process, for all people living under it, not just citizens. It comes complete with the mechanisms in place that will let us save it, if we are willing.

IF THAT'S THE SHOT, HERE'S THE CHASER: WITHOUT DEMOCRACY IN place as the architecture for our society, it becomes far more difficult to make progress on the issues we care about. Take climate change. It's an understatement to say that it has been difficult enough as is to get government to address it in a sustained way. Imagine trying to address climate issues if, instead of a president and parties who face reelection, government is solidly entrenched in the hands of big business and a billionaire class. You don't really have to imagine it. You can observe what has happened in an America where a president who seizes reins of power he is not intended to hold kneecaps the Environmental Protection Agency and guts its work, while also defunding academic institutions that supplement the government's work by conducting research or programs designed to reduce the impact of climate change. Because we live in a democracy, if Americans who care deeply about these issues participate in the political process in significant numbers, these decisions can be reversed. That doesn't mean the Trump administration won't do significant damage in the meantime. But they do not have to be the last word.

THE MESSY PROCESS OF DEMOCRACY

Late in President Barack Obama's second term in office, the United States became one of the original signatories to the Paris Agreement. Signed by 195 parties in 2015, the Paris Agreement was a pact to reduce global greenhouse gas emissions in order to limit worldwide temperature increases. In 2017, Trump tried to withdraw from the Paris Agreement. He failed, but only because back then there was a four-year time-line in place for a withdrawal to go into effect. On his first day in office in 2021, President Biden reupped the United States' commitment to participate in that global effort before the withdrawal could be finalized. The Biden administration set new targets and made a commitment to reach net-zero emissions by 2050. Despite the host of other day-one priorities Biden faced, rejoining the Paris Agreement was at the top of the list.

That's the value of a democratic system where periodic elections allow voters to determine priorities by virtue of the people they elect. Elected representatives, at least in some part, are accountable to the voters and must deliver on what the people who elected them want. Was rejoining the Paris Agreement everything voters concerned about climate change had in mind? No. But it was a commitment Biden might not have made but for the need to be responsive to a significant political constituency. That's democracy in action, and the return to the Paris Agreement was a floor, not a ceiling, for what America could do.

In January 2025, as soon as he took office for a second time, Trump withdrew from the Paris Agreement again. The Agreement now permits Trump to withdraw US support for it just one year after indicating he intends to do so. He got straight to it in an executive order titled "President Trump's America First Priorities." Elections have consequences.

The back-and-forth damages our global stature. But, of course, it is the effort to deal with the effects of climate change that really suffers. Trump's executive order on the subject announced that "the President will unleash American energy by ending Biden's policies of climate extremism, streamlining permitting, and reviewing for rescission all regulations that impose undue burdens on energy production and use, including mining and processing of non-fuel minerals." "I'm immediately withdrawing from the unfair, one-sided Paris climate accord rip-off," Trump said. Game over.

This is not just partisan politics. Trump behaved like a leader who no longer feels the tug of democracy. Earlier Republican administrations at least gestured toward climate change solutions, although in ways many Americans believed were insufficient. But as authoritarians separate from the democratic process, voters, even their own voters, have a severely constrained ability to influence them. They act with their own interests in mind. Abandoning democracy means opting out of representative government and into the world of autocracy. Even the prospect of progress, let alone progress itself, gets taken off the table. In essence, we go backward, because rulers don't care about what matters to their subjects. We abandon democracy at our literal peril.

While climate change is an important example, there are so many other pressing issues that need to be attended to. The specifics vary, but the point remains the same. In a democracy, the people elect government officials, and if those officials want to stay in office, they must be responsive to the people's concerns. In effect, voters who understand democracy know that they have the responsibility for shaping government. But our work doesn't end when we elect officials.

There must also be an ongoing process of directing them while they're in office. Decades of taking democracy for granted mean we've slipped away from this model of government, which was so important in the view of the Founding Fathers—a government by, for, and of the people. Reminding *our* elected officials that no matter what party they belong to, they represent us, and they serve at our pleasure, is something all of us can participate in. And we must be willing to back that up with hard work come election time. A cloud descends over democracy when people give up, and it leads us to relinquish the feeling that we are entitled, even obligated, to demand good government from our elected officials. We succumb to the belief they won't listen to us and that our voices don't matter. We give up. But that's *not* how a democracy works.

Democracy forces leaders to consider citizens' views. Whatever issues you care about the most—criminal justice reform, affordable housing, climate change, education, international relations, or others—progress is more likely in the presence of a robust democracy, especially if the problems you worry about don't impact the ruling class. Why have a democracy? So that you matter.

The reality is that while governing is hard work, without it we have chaos. And with it we can make progress. The promise of democracy is not a fiction. But it does require people who are committed to good government and good works working together. Giving up out of exasperation with imperfection isn't the answer that's best for us in the short run or the long run. On a pragmatic level, and as Americans have painfully learned in the last few years, nothing leaves us worse off than abandoning democracy.

PAINFUL GROWTH AND CIVIL RIGHTS

In June 1963, Alabama's segregationist governor George Wallace made his infamous stand in the schoolhouse door, literally trying to bar the path to court-ordered integration at the University of Alabama in Tuscaloosa. Six months earlier, in January, Wallace, in his inaugural address, had promised Alabama voters "segregation now, segregation tomorrow, segregation forever." Under pressure from Washington, DC, to follow court orders, Wallace ultimately stepped aside after President John F. Kennedy federalized National Guardsmen, who accompanied two Black students, Vivian Malone Jones and James Hood, into Foster Auditorium at the university so that they could register for summer school.

James Hood was born in Gadsden, Alabama, in 1942. His father drove a tractor at the Goodyear Tire factory that, decades later, would spawn Lilly Ledbetter's fight for equal pay for women. He started his education at Clark College, now Clark Atlanta University, an HBCU (one of the nation's historically Black colleges and universities) in Georgia. But Hood wanted to transfer to Alabama to study clinical psychology, which Clark didn't offer. He dreamed of countering discriminatory work in the field, like claims Black people's brain development was inferior to whites'.

Hood left the university after only a few months in order

to avoid what he later called "complete mental and physical breakdown" brought on by the stress of being part of the forced integration. After his agonizing first day on campus, Hood was forced to live alone. He was the sole student occupant of a dorm floor he shared only with deputy US marshals who were there to protect him. Hood transferred to Wayne State, in Michigan, where he received his bachelor's degree. Almost thirty-five years later, he returned to the University of Alabama, completing his doctorate in 1997.

Vivian Malone Jones stayed on campus and went on to become the first Black person to graduate from the university, in May 1965. She had grown up in Mobile, Alabama, and received a bachelor's degree from Alabama A&M, another HBCU. But A&M lost its accreditation, and she set her sights on attending the University of Alabama to receive an accredited degree. Her struggle to enroll revealed the senselessness of segregation: An honor student, Malone Jones was rejected, she was told, due to "class size" and "enrollment issues." She persevered, showing extraordinary courage during her time on campus. In a 2004 interview with the *Post-Standard* of Syracuse, she recounted the day in November 1963 when four bombs went off, one just a few blocks from her residence. "I decided not to show any fear and went to classes that day," she said. After she graduated, Malone Jones went on to work in the Justice Department's Civil Rights Division. When the university commemorated integration fifty years later, her younger sister Sharon's husband, Eric Holder, was the first Black attorney general of the United States.

James Hood and Vivian Malone Jones, at great personal

cost, forced the system to work for them at a time when it might have seemed easier to let it burn down. Their courage forced Governor Wallace to literally walk away from segregation. They chose democracy and a path that permitted tens of thousands of other young men and women to follow them into the halls of higher education. Let's not pretend it was fair, or easy, or perfect, or that the progress always followed a linear path. It didn't. But still, there is a direct line between the first Black college student at the University of Alabama and the first Black attorney general of the United States.

Instead of giving up on democracy because its promise wasn't extended to include them, Hood and Malone Jones chose to fight to expand its promise. The courts, along with a willing president, moved us forward during the civil rights era. Sometimes it has been Congress, sometimes the courts, sometimes a president, sometimes a combination of the three. And we *have* made progress. One need only look back over the long arc of history in a country where people were once enslaved, where women couldn't vote, where Jews and Catholics were barely tolerated, and where so many other offenses were committed against the dignity of human beings that it would take another book to list them all. It's easy to criticize a society's flaws and what it has left to do; the places where it hasn't yet succeeded. But it's important to also acknowledge how much we've accomplished, and that still more is possible.

Part of the problem is this: Progress doesn't always come easily, and when we make it, it doesn't always stick. Sometimes we stop making progress. And in recent years, it's frequently felt like we're not even treading water; we're going backward.

THE IMPERFECT SUPREME COURT

The courts can break your heart. The same Supreme Court that can make positive changes once thought near impossible can also extinguish them. After decades of gains made possible by cases it decided, in 2023 the Supreme Court struck down affirmative action in education, and potentially more broadly. In *Students for Fair Admissions v. Harvard* and *Students for Fair Admissions v. University of North Carolina*, the Court ended the use of race as one among a number of criteria for college admissions. This laid the groundwork for the second Trump administration to target diversity, equity, and inclusion (DEI) programs, and not just in schools. By executive order, the president prohibited government offices from considering race, gender, and other diversity factors when making employment and policy decisions. The new administration tried to impose its views on private businesses, including law firms and government contractors, and colleges and universities as well, using the withholding of government funding and contracts to whitewash history under the pretense that discrimination had no lingering effects. Progress is a fragile thing; it can easily slip away. It's easy to understand why people might lose faith in democracy if all they can see is the present.

Our recent history is not the only time the Supreme

Court has utterly failed to meet the moment. In a notorious 1857 case, *Dred Scott v. Sandford*, the Supreme Court decided that no matter whether they were free or enslaved, Black people were not and could not be American citizens. The judges held that Congress couldn't prohibit slavery. In the majority opinion, Chief Justice Roger B. Taney wrote these scarring words about Black Americans: "They had for more than a century before been regarded as beings of an inferior order . . . either in social or political relations; and so far inferior, that they had no rights which the white man was bound to respect; and that the negro might justly and lawfully be reduced to slavery for his benefit."

The case started out in state court in Missouri. Dred Scott and his wife, Harriet, who were enslaved, sued for their freedom in St. Louis Circuit Court in 1846. They argued that because they had lived in free territory with the people who enslaved them for a period of years, they had been emancipated. Their theory was "once free, always free." It seemed like common sense. A person residing in an area where slavery was illegal could not be enslaved. Once they had been freed, there was no provision of law that provided for re-enslavement. Missouri's courts had used similar facts to free other enslaved people, holding that once they lived in free territory, they remained free, even if returned to slave territory.

According to the Supreme Court, the defendant in the case, John Sandford, purchased Dred Scott, Harriet, and their two daughters, Eliza and Lizzie, from an army surgeon at Fort Snelling, Minnesota. When they sued, Sandford fought them in court for eleven years, first in state court, and then in a federal case that was argued twice before the US Supreme Court. The Supreme Court said the question before it was simply this: "Can a negro whose ancestors were imported into this country, and sold as slaves, become a member of the political community formed and brought into existence by the Constitution of the United States, and as such become entitled to all the rights and privileges and immunities guaranteed to the citizen? One of which rights is the privilege of suing in a court of the United States in the cases specified in the Constitution?" To our nation's everlasting shame, the Court said the answer was no.

Looking for a reason to reject a system of government because of systemic racial inequity? There it is. But here's the thing about democracy: Having three branches of government means that when one fails, there is opportunity for the others to rise to the occasion. This was an extreme situation; a bloody Civil War took place before the wrong was remedied. And it was ultimately Congress, with ratification from the states, that remedied the great evil of the *Dred Scott* case, passing the amendments to the Constitution that abolished slavery, granted citizenship, and created voting rights.

Our country has never fully reckoned with the great evil of slavery. That is still ahead of us. But Congress's work set the stage for the Supreme Court to collect itself and issue subsequent rulings that guaranteed and expanded civil rights, including, in 1954, the Supreme Court's landmark decision in *Brown v. Board of Education*, in which the Court held it wasn't enough to have schools that were (supposedly) "separate but equal." The Supreme Court ruled that integration was required. *Brown* set us on the path for James Hood and Vivian Malone Jones to walk into Foster Auditorium and advance the struggle to dismantle segregation, despite opposition from people like George Wallace. When the courts failed the country, Congress and the president acted. At other times, it's the courts that keep democracy on track. When one branch of government is out of whack, our system is designed so that another branch can keep us afloat until our balance can be restored.

Our system may not always function as we would hope and expect, but with hard work and diligence, we can continue to move forward. The chaos that would come with rejecting democracy, opening up a vacuum an autocrat could step into, would halt progress—the will of the people would be replaced with the whims of a dictatorial leader. Compare that to the at times frustratingly slow pace, but possibility-laden prospect, of working to improve democracy, and the choice seems clear.

One final example underscores the reasons for sticking it out, even when it seems like democracy may not be up to the task. The Supreme Court failed the country again when it decided *Korematsu v. United States* in 1944. Two years earlier, President Franklin D. Roosevelt issued Executive Order 9066, authorizing the internment of Japanese Americans during World War II. One hundred twenty thousand Americans living on the West Coast were ripped out of their homes and communities and forcibly sent to internment camps. Roosevelt sought to justify the move by citing a need to protect national security. He also invoked the Alien Enemies Act. All immigrants of Japanese descent who were over the age of fourteen were declared "alien enemies," even though there was never any evidence of sabotage.

Fred Korematsu was born in Oakland, California, in 1919. His family fell under Executive Order 9066. He refused to comply, was arrested, and was sent to the stockade in San Francisco. The ACLU got wind of Korematsu's plight and one of their lawyers showed up to see him. Korematsu decided to challenge his conviction and fight his arrest.

The Supreme Court affirmed Korematsu's conviction and the internment orders in a 6–3 decision on December 18, 1944. By this time, he had been permitted to rejoin his family in Detroit, where they were starting over as part of a wave of Japanese Americans who had been able to secure jobs outside the West Coast. It was a dark moment in American history, stripping thousands of people of their homes, businesses, communities, and rights, and it took decades to even come close to righting the wrong. In 1988, Congress passed the Civil Liberties Act, which provided reparations and a formal apology to surviving internees. In 2018, a majority of the Supreme Court, in *Trump v. Hawaii*, finally repudiated *Korematsu*, although they didn't explicitly overrule it. Ironically, that case involved Trump's first-term travel ban on predominately Muslim countries. Justices Ruth Bader Ginsburg and Sonia Sotomayor, in dissent, criticized the majority for permitting another racist policy, disguised in the clothing of "a barren invocation of national security," to survive, calling the parallels between their case and *Korematsu* "stark." In response, Chief Justice John Roberts wrote that the majority acknowledged that what was done to Japanese Americans was "objectively unlawful and outside the scope of Presidential authority." Although the conservative majority signed off on the Muslim ban, which they held prohibited "certain foreign nationals the privilege of admission," they did reject *Korematsu*. The language is important: "*Korematsu* was gravely wrong the day it was decided, has been overruled in the court of history, and—to be clear—'has no place in law under the Constitution.'"

Sometimes progress is, in effect, forced, as it was in that case, or when President Kennedy forced Governor Wallace to step aside. Sometimes the push comes from Congress, which passed the civil rights law that made that day in Alabama possible. Sometimes progress happens in the Court, even if it is delayed or flawed, as with the undoing of *Korematsu*. We should not lose sight of the fact that the public plays a role in progress too. The details of what had for too many years been a private shame for Japanese Americans—some members of Fred Korematsu's own family didn't want him to challenge internment in court—were increasingly made public. Children's books and essays, including by well-known actor and activist George Takei, the *Star Trek* star whose family experienced internment, drove a public conversation about the injustice. We are doomed to repeat mistakes if we don't learn from them. Each of the three branches of government is capable of rejuvenating democracy when it fails. Citizens—all of us—do that too.

There is no denying that ours is a system founded in racial inequality, where enslavement was lawful and Black people counted as three-fifths of a person in our founding documents. Women had no rights to vote or hold property at all. Evolving out of injustice, rather than drowning in it, is the real story of democracy. We are a country foundationally capable of evolving, but it is hard and often painful work. And it can take time. It is still better than the alternatives.

LAWS AND POLICIES THAT PUSHED US TOWARD GREATER EQUALITY in education have moved the country forward, expanding the pool of talented Americans who are able to fully participate in our society. Affirmative action policies played a significant role. When more kids can see teachers, astronauts, politicians, and lawyers who look like them, it opens up a world of possibilities. In 2023, when the Supreme Court rolled that back in the pair of cases that rejected considerations of race as one of multiple factors in making admissions decisions and found that Harvard and the University of North Carolina's admissions programs violated the Equal Protection Clause of the Fourteenth Amendment, Donald Trump applauded. He posted his reaction to the decisions on social media.

"We're going back," he wrote.

Justice Ketanji Brown Jackson's dissent in the University of North Carolina case spoke loudly: "Gulf-sized race-based gaps exist with respect to the health, wealth, and well-being of American citizens. They were created in the distant past, but have indisputably been passed down to the present day through the generations. Every moment these gaps persist is a moment in which this great country falls short of actualizing one of its foundational principles—the 'self-evident' truth that all of us are created equal." And then, her ringing criticism of the majority opinion: "Deeming race irrelevant in law does not make it so in life."

It's easy to reject what's imperfect and walk away from it. It's more difficult to acknowledge the imperfections and commit to fixing them. As New Jersey Senator Cory Booker tweeted back in 2018 and reiterated in his monumental twenty-five-hour 2025 filibuster against Trump's assaults on democracy, "If this country hasn't broken your heart, you probably don't love Her enough." It's hard to imagine truer words, given the last decade of American history. We have kids, now young adults, whose earliest experience of the presidency is Donald Trump's first term in office. There are people who believe democracy is fundamentally broken. To come back from this place, it's important that as we discuss democracy, we are cognizant of this new need to make the case not just for policies we believe in but for democracy itself, and for making the commitment to keep improving it.

This moment is unique because it is not a single Supreme Court case or a single political issue that we are worried about. It's an all-out attack on democracy, launched by our own president. That possibility wasn't on anyone's bingo card a decade ago. It's still shocking. But even in dire circumstances, the principle for keeping the Republic remains the same. Look for the institution that will hold and provide resilience until the balance of power can be restored and the country set aright. Make sure the public is critically engaged. The scope of this problem is bigger than any the country has faced in decades, but that's no reason to give up.

How do you eat an elephant? One bite at a time. George Wallace was forced to step aside in 1963. The conservatives on the Supreme Court eventually recanted *Korematsu*. We can do it again. It takes hope and persistence in equal measure, and a stubborn refusal to give up. It's individual Americans who come together, and their resolve, that sustain a democracy through dark times. You have a voice. You have a vote. They matter. If they didn't matter, people who don't want democracy to continue wouldn't be working so hard to take them away from you. Hug that knowledge close and put it to good use.

GOOD TROUBLE AND SELMA

America's history is replete with examples of Americans using their power for good. Efforts to secure the right to vote for Black citizens came to a head in Selma, Alabama, on Bloody Sunday, March 7, 1965. Jim Clark, the sheriff in Dallas County, where Selma is located, was deeply opposed to letting Black people vote. His opposition included refusing entry to 105 Black teachers who had lined up neatly down the Dallas County courthouse steps and along the sidewalk outside, two by two, careful to not block anyone else's access as they waited patiently to register to vote. Georgia Congressman John Lewis recounted the kinds of literacy tests Black people were subjected to in order to prevent them from voting during that time. "On one occasion," Lewis said years later, "a man was asked to count the number of bubbles on a bar soap. On another occasion, a man was asked to count the number of jelly beans in a jar." White voters in the state, needless to say, did not have to pass these sorts of nonsensical and offensive examinations in order to register to vote. There was also outright intimidation, and there was violence against people who tried to support the teachers by supplying them with food and water while they stood in long lines.

On March 7, a group of marchers, Black and white, left Brown Chapel AME Church in Selma, taking their first steps in what they expected would be a peaceful march to Alabama's capitol in Montgomery. In events that are now well-known, they approached the Edmund Pettus Bridge. Singing and marching, they were met by state troopers, some mounted on horses, who used clubs and tear gas to stop the march. Many people, including John Lewis, whose skull was fractured, were grievously injured. Two days later they returned, on Turnaround Tuesday, in a march led by Martin Luther King Jr., where they went to the bridge and knelt in prayer but did not attempt to cross it.

Then Judge Frank M. Johnson, a federal judge in Montgomery, issued an injunction that required state troopers to stop interfering with the marchers. In a Solomonic ruling, he went further and required the troopers to protect them. Judge Johnson wasn't new to the civil rights fights that had spilled into the courts across the South. He had already ruled (along with another judge) against the city of Montgomery in its fight to keep buses segregated, affirming the victory of Rosa Parks and the Montgomery bus boycotters. Judge Johnson went on to issue court orders that forced the inclusion of Black citizens on voter rolls, required statewide school desegregation for the first time, and prohibited discrimination in public places like Alabama's libraries and transportation centers.

Wallace, who had been Judge Johnson's classmate at the University of Alabama, called him an "integrating, scalawagging, carpetbagging liar." But Judge Johnson, who had seen the footage from Bloody Sunday on CBS Television, held firm. Under his court-ordered protection, marchers left Brown Chapel for a third time, on Sunday, March 25, 1965, for the fifty-mile march from Selma to Montgomery. By the time they reached Montgomery, they were more than twenty-five thousand people strong.

A system that was steeped in racism and had failed Black voters for far too long began to work at long last—the courts and citizens insisted on it; the president and Congress played supporting roles. Democracy worked.

Sustaining our system of democracy requires courage and doesn't come without cost. Viola Liuzzo, a white mom of five from Michigan, was among the marchers. A longtime crusader for civil rights, she had come to Montgomery to help secure the right to vote for people she didn't know but nonetheless cared about deeply. As she drove one of the protesters, a young Black man, between Selma and Montgomery, a carload of Klansmen pulled up alongside them. Liuzzo tried to speed past them, but a Klansman pulled a gun and shot her point-blank in the head, killing her. Despite predictable efforts to smear her name, she is one of the heroes of the movement, a woman who did what was right, despite fierce opposition and the price she ended up paying. She marched in the crowd that included John Lewis, and despite the tragedy of her death, while she was alive, she made what he famously—throughout his long career—called "good trouble." Good trouble. In an era when far too many people become engaged only when issues touch their lives, the example set by Viola Liuzzo is an important one: Help other people. Their rights are every bit as important as your own.

A YEAR AND A HALF BEFORE THE MARCH ACROSS THE EDMUND Pettus Bridge, on a steamy August day in Washington, Dr. Martin Luther King Jr. climbed the steps of the Lincoln Memorial to give a speech that, as much as any other, would come to define his remarkable life. A quarter million of his fellow Americans filled the National Mall below him. The address would echo across years for its vision, for Dr. King's *dream*. But I turn back to it for his answer to our central question: Why not just give up on democracy because of its imperfections?

Dr. King said, "When the architects of our republic wrote the magnificent words of the Constitution and the Declaration of Independence, they were signing a promissory note to which every American was to fall heir. This note was a promise that all men, yes, black men as well as white men, would be guaranteed the unalienable rights of life, liberty, and the pursuit of happiness." He went on to say that it had become "obvious" that "America has defaulted on this promissory note insofar as her citizens of color are concerned." Even though our government had not achieved its promise, he rejected the idea that democracy itself was flawed, telling the crowd that he did not believe that "the bank of justice is bankrupt."

Hopelessness is where autocrats try to push you so that you'll stop opposing them. The answer? Be like Dr. King. Be like Viola Liuzzo. Be like John Lewis. Be like Frank Johnson. Be like George Takei. Refuse to give up. Don't let anyone convince you that democracy isn't worth fighting for because it contains flaws, even serious ones. Without democracy, we wouldn't have a shot at fixing them.

CHAPTER 4

A New Lost Cause

January 6, 2021. All those who witnessed the events of that horrible day will never forget them. Even as the precise details of the unfolding attack on the Capitol fade, that dawning sense of horror remains. As we watched and listened, we realized that we were in the middle of an attempted coup, intended to interfere with the transfer of power from one duly elected president to another, for the first time in our nation's history.

No one put it better than leading Senate Republican Mitch McConnell of Kentucky, who—after Trump was impeached by the House and acquitted by the Senate—called Trump's conduct on January 6 "disgraceful" and said that Trump was "practically and morally responsible" for what took place. House GOP minority leader Kevin McCarthy said Trump's behavior on January 6 was "atrocious and totally wrong" in a

January 8 call with other key Republicans, although he never went that far in public. He did accuse Trump of "inciting" the mob that went to the Capitol. McConnell and McCarthy were not alone. Other Republicans who had feared for their lives on January 6 joined in as well. But their outrage, or perhaps their supply of courage, was short-lived.

Written for MSNBC just a few days after January 6, my real-time assessment was that the commitment of the acting U.S. Attorney in Washington, DC, to prosecute every case of wrongdoing, while laudable, was misguided. I argued that what the country needed in the moment was "clarity and a focus on the real threat: the ongoing risk posed by the people who conspired to overthrow the government and were willing to resort to violence to do it." Unfortunately, we never got there. There were hundreds of prosecutions of people who overran the Capitol, now all pardoned by Trump. There were a handful of more serious cases alleging seditious conspiracy, mostly pardoned now as well. Donald Trump was indicted, too, but the cases against him have been dismissed or sidelined by virtue of his reelection. There was never any accountability at the top. That moment of national reckoning, where the country pointed a finger at itself and acknowledged the ongoing issues we couldn't wish away, never came. We cannot change how these events played out, but we can draw upon our powerful national history and use it for guidance and inspiration in moving forward despite them. In many ways, the moment we live in is unique, but history and culture, especially our literature, can provide inspiration if we turn to them.

One caveat as we embark upon this chapter, which draws heavily on American history: I am a lawyer by training, not a historian. But like many Americans, I am deeply interested in and curious about our nation's past, especially where it intersects with the law. And that connection is particularly poignant when it comes to prior instances of insurrection in the United States, most notably the Civil War. It is hard to ignore the resonance between that mass treason and the events that concluded the first Trump administration. History may not repeat, but as Mark Twain is credited with pointing out, it does rhyme.

THE LATE UNPLEASANTNESS

The first shots of the American Civil War were fired at Fort Sumter on April 12, 1861. On April 9, 1865, even before the war ended, the process of granting amnesty and pardons to Confederates who were willing to swear loyalty to the United States and abandon slavery was underway. In December 1863, President Lincoln issued the Proclamation of Amnesty and Reconstruction, a safe harbor that was available to most people, with the exception of high-ranking Confederate officials and people who had mistreated Black soldiers. Reentry into the American fold required an oath, which read as follows:

> I do solemnly swear in presence of Almighty God, that I will henceforth faithfully support, protect, and defend the Constitution of the United States, and the

Union of the States thereunder; and that I will, in like manner, abide by, and faithfully support all Acts of Congress passed during the existing rebellion, with reference to slaves, so long, and so far, as not repealed, modified, or held void by Congress, or by decision of the Supreme Court; and that I will, in like manner, abide by and faithfully support, all proclamations of the President made during the existing rebellion, having reference to slaves, so long, and so far as not modified, or declared void by decision of the Supreme Court, so help me God.

It was a generous forgiveness. Congress didn't like it, but Lincoln persisted. After the final surrender at Appomattox, Confederate soldiers were allowed to return home, "paroled" and free from the threat of prosecution, so long as they remained law-abiding.

Five days after the Confederate surrender at Appomattox, Lincoln was dead at the hands of an assassin. He was replaced by his vice president, Andrew Johnson, a Tennessee Democrat who himself had purchased and enslaved at least three people until August 1863. Johnson, personally sympathetic to the former Confederates' cause, expanded Lincoln's clemency further in a series of additional orders. By December 1868, Johnson was ready to issue universal amnesty. He explained away earlier limits on pardons that had excluded high-ranking Confederates as necessary so close in time to the war because of "prudential reservations and exceptions." But now there was no longer any reason for them, he said, concluding they "were deemed necessary and proper [then, but] may now be wisely and justly relinquished." Johnson proclaimed universal amnesty and a pardon for everyone involved in the "rebellion." It would "tend to secure permanent peace, order, and prosperity throughout the land," he believed, "and to renew and fully restore confidence and fraternal feeling among the whole people, and their respect for and attachment to the National Government."

There is always tension between the desire for justice and the hope of reconciliation. We need not debate the wisdom, or lack of it, in Johnson's approach. It cannot be changed now. It preserved the Union but left issues of race largely unacknowledged and unaddressed, hastening the backtracking of Reconstruction into Jim Crow. The question of how best to heal a nation and keep the Republic without setting an unacceptably low bar of accountability for those who failed to honor the Constitution is a difficult one. But no interests are served by glossing over the truth, back then as now.

In addition to the humiliating defeat he suffered, Jefferson Davis went to prison after the Civil War, although only for two years. General Robert E. Lee, who had lost his citizenship as the leader of the Confederate Army, applied to President Johnson for a pardon in 1865, as Johnson was testing the waters with a series of decrees on the path to offering total amnesty. It was after one of them that Lee initially applied for a pardon, ultimately signing the oath of loyalty under Johnson's full order of amnesty. But it wasn't until over a century later, after an archivist uncovered Lee's lost Amnesty Oath, that Congress voted to restore his full rights of citizenship.

Forgiveness comes easier, and has fewer consequences, one hundred years after the fact. Following January 6, emotions ran high but there was no moment when Donald Trump faced the truth about what he had done to the country. He has never publicly apologized or even acknowledged he was wrong. There was no moment like the surrender at Appomattox or the withholding of restoration of citizenship. Trump's supporters who participated in January 6 were prosecuted, many of them pleading guilty to crimes committed on his behalf, but he never faced a jury. Trump never offered his side of the story in a courtroom, so a jury could determine the truth and render a verdict. That's no way to fix a democracy and keep it whole.

Of course, hindsight is twenty-twenty, and it is easier to be forgiving when all the participants are long dead. Near the close of the Civil War, President Lincoln made a list of generals who should be imprisoned for treason, but that never came to pass. Writing in 2014, Penn State historian William Blair noted the irony of leniency, which made it easier for Confederate generals like Lee to become heroes to later generations. Blair cited the words of Union General George Thomas, who wrote in 1868 that "the crime of treason might be covered with a counterfeit varnish of patriotism, so that the precipitators of the rebellion might go down in history hand-in-hand with the defenders of the [US] Government." Even if the intention was merely to hold the country together, ignoring the risk posed by the very same people who conspired to overthrow the government and were willing to resort to violence to do it cannot be a path forward.

In the wake of the Civil War, the fiction of "the Lost Cause" grew in Southern mythology. The term was coined by Virginian Edward Alfred Pollard, who advocated for slavery before the war and tried to justify the Confederacy afterward in his 1866 book, *The Lost Cause: A New Southern History of the War of the Confederates*. The Lost Cause became a way for Southerners to recast treason and rebellion as a principled conflict over states' rights, their battle a righteous one for their highly romanticized version of plantation life and slavery. These were and are the fictions that have allowed a resurgence of white supremacy, including slogans like "It's heritage, not hate."

THE MORE RECENT UNPLEASANTNESS

The problem our country faced after January 6 was in part legal and in part political. It should have been addressed directly in both venues, particularly while Democrats in Congress had the votes to lead the way. It was an abdication of responsibility to wait for the criminal justice system to address the threat the country continued to face after January 6 when the political solution, impeachment, was at hand. When Trump left the White House, the culture he created didn't go away. With no closure and in the absence of accountability for January 6, Trump was free to rewrite the story into a Lost Cause mythology of his own, complete with *true patriots*—the guys in masks who attacked police officers, defecated in the Capitol, and threatened to hang Vice President Mike Pence. Senate Republicans failed to hold Trump accountable. They could have removed him from office at the end of his first term and foreclosed the prospect he would ever run again. But they flinched when the moment called for courage. Conviction in the Senate on impeachment charges requires a two-thirds majority of those present. Trump was acquitted 57–43, with only seven Republicans crossing over to vote in favor of conviction.

Days after the insurrection, Mitch McConnell privately reassured advisors that "the Democrats are going to take care of the son of a bitch for us," a reference to the impeachment. Democrats were willing to lead, but Republicans failed to muster the handful of votes necessary to finish the job. Republican senators offered reason after reason the Senate couldn't convict and claimed that someone else should hold Trump accountable. McConnell suggested the criminal justice system could take care of Trump. (The Supreme Court turned out to have a different idea.) Iowa Senator Chuck Grassley, the ranking Republican on the Senate Judiciary Committee, opined that the Senate didn't have the ability to try a *former* president, which meant that by delaying proceedings for a couple of weeks, they gave Trump an out. Utah Senator Mike Lee blamed the Democrats for failing to prove their case and for delaying the proceedings until Trump was out of office. In truth, Senate Republicans pushed for the delay, but Senate Democrats, trying to figure out how they would operate with their new 51–50 majority (including the vice president as tiebreaker), did not push either.

And so, like most Confederate leaders, Donald Trump escaped accountability in the political arena. A few years later he would do the same in the courts. Then-President Joe Biden put it most eloquently of all, speaking on the third anniversary of January 6 near Valley Forge, Pennsylvania, where General Washington and his troops endured a long, cold winter during the Revolutionary War. He simply said of that day, "We nearly lost America—lost it all." My view, the view of a prosecutor, is that it's important to prosecute the people most responsible for a serious crime. And this was one of the most serious imaginable. It's up to a jury to decide whether to convict or not, but if they don't have the opportunity, justice hasn't been done. If our most powerful leaders can't be held accountable when they violate the law, people's confidence in the rule of law wavers. It becomes nearly impossible for the country to learn the lesson and move forward.

But it doesn't have to end that way.

THE ATTACK ON JANUARY 6 SHOULD HAVE BEEN ANTICIPATED. That's law enforcement's job. At best, leaders were unprepared. At worst, they succumbed to an unforgivable bias that said folks who looked so much like them couldn't be dangerous. As a result, the people's house was left vulnerable. Law enforcement failed to appreciate and prepare for a threat that was readily apparent to anyone who perused pro-Trump chat rooms and message boards on 4chan and other sites.

That failure is past. It is now the jurisdiction of historians. Our energy is better spent on the threat itself and the people who created it. Because that threat has not dissipated; it has morphed and perhaps grown stronger. Now we see the consequences of preserving the fiction that all the people on both sides of the political divide were operating in good faith. You can be polite to everyone, or you can save the Republic. But you cannot do both.

We can, however, summon our courage and be fearless in the face of the bully. We have to be unafraid to say out loud that there are people in our country who didn't value the Constitution and our laws, didn't honor our tradition of democracy, of fairness, of justice, of inclusion, and wanted to rewrite the rules of the Republic to suit themselves. History can help us understand how to deal with this threat. As FDR said in 1941, when appeasement was suggested as an alternative to joining the fight against foreign tyrants:

> As a nation, we may take pride in the fact that we are softhearted; but we cannot afford to be soft-headed. We must always be wary of those who with sounding brass and a tinkling cymbal preach the "ism" of appeasement. We must especially beware of that small group of selfish men who would clip the wings of the American eagle in order to feather their own nests.

THE HISTORY OF THE RULE OF LAW

A dive into the history of the rule of law clarifies why the Founding Fathers saw it as the architecture that the Constitution was built upon. That history can also inform us about how the rule of law can operate as the bulwark against those who, in FDR's words, would clip the eagle's wings. When the rule of law is in place and healthy, a country has laws that everyone knows (or at least has public access to) and those laws are applied fairly to everyone. In his 2010 book, *The Rule of Law*, Sir Thomas Bingham wrote that, at bottom, the rule of law provides much-needed predictability in the conduct of our lives and businesses. Jeremy Waldron, an NYU law professor who studies the rule of law, puts it like this: "People value the Rule of Law because it takes some of the edge off the power that is necessarily exercised over them in a political community. In various ways, being ruled through law, means that power is less arbitrary, more predictable, more impersonal, less peremptory, less coercive even."

The rule of law is not an abstract concept. It has strong practical effects on our daily lives. The powerful can't steal with impunity from those who are weaker. They can't take your home, your car, or your kids away from you. They can't use your creations, your intellectual property, without permission. Our employers have a legally enforceable obligation to pay us for our work because of the rule of law. Your landlord can't suddenly evict you because of the rule of law. People understand that there are set rules that govern our interactions with others, falling under both civil law and criminal law. The rule of law is one of the reasons that people from other countries have felt comfortable making investments in the United States in past decades: A stable rule of law society protects even foreign investors' interests. This is the practical, daily import of the rule of law, which stabilizes society for people who are more interested in business than in politics or law—whether they realize it or not.

Unlike legal terms with precise meaning—"due process" or "equal protection"—there isn't a single, commonly used definition of the rule of law. To Waldron, the "Rule of Law is one of the ideals of our political morality and it refers to the ascendancy of law as such and of the institutions of the legal system in a system of governance." Less formally, it means that people who live under a rule of law system are protected by the law because everyone, including government officials and government offices, has to follow it. In a rule of law system, people know what the law *is*—and its strictures are enforced against all people, administered by an independent judiciary. No kings. As we once said with certainty, no man is above the law.

Donald Trump, from the start of his first term in office, acted as though the rule of law didn't apply to him. He retained control of his business interests. His namesake hotel in Washington, DC, became a watering hole for people seeking connections—one of the many indications that he was not concerned with the Emoluments Clauses of the Constitution, which prohibit a president from using his office for personal financial gain. He permitted people in his administration to violate the Hatch Act, which restricts political activity by government employees, without consequence. Rejecting the rule of law is no small act; it is a fundamental attack on our way of life. When a president can bring the full power of the executive branch to bear on people and entities he perceives as his personal enemies, then the law, by definition, is not being applied to everyone equally. It is government by whim. The level of uncertainty in our communities reverberates broadly.

The English philosopher John Locke, in his seminal 1689 volume *Two Treatises of Government*, emphasized that the public had to know what the law *actually says* for the rule of law to work. That seems an obvious point today when we have written laws readily available on the internet and in libraries. But Locke wrote in an era when the law was more capricious and advance notice of what conduct could be deemed criminal was less certain. He wrote that "established standing laws, promulgated and known to the people," were critical, contrasting them with a government that ruled through "extemporary arbitrary decrees."

By "arbitrary," Locke meant laws that were unclear and might be applied in unexpected ways. His view was that a ruler behaved arbitrarily if he imposed rules with no notice, making up the law as he went along. That approach left the ruler's subjects adrift as they attempted to conduct their daily affairs. The only thing that was predictable was the arbitrary nature of the world around them. As Locke put it, without the rule of law, people are subject to a king, a despot if you will, who forces them to live with "sudden thoughts, or unrestrained, and till that moment unknown wills [of the ruler] without having any measures set down which may guide and justify their actions." To Locke, predictability and certainty were essential for people to live together in community. It made sense in the 1600s and it makes sense today.

What are a citizen's obligations in a rule of law system? At the most basic, each of us must follow the rules or prepare to be held accountable if we choose to violate them, even laws we don't agree with. In a functioning rule of law system, everyone is protected equally because they are able to know what the law is, so they can understand what they are obligated to do (and refrain from doing), and they know how they will be treated by authorities if they are involved in civil disagreements or break the law. It's a framework that lets people live and prosper together without resorting to violence, Hatfield and McCoy–style, to resolve every dispute. The rule of law is something we simultaneously take for granted and can't live without.

All this illuminates the seismic shift of Trumpism. It illustrates why presidents shouldn't exceed their constitutional powers and why courts and Congress should act expeditiously to hold them accountable when they do. If the rule of law fails, it's not just pretty words; we lose the bedrock of stability that protects our way of life.

Re-anchoring the rule of law in America will require more than the involvement of lawyers and politicians. Public understanding of the rule of law—what it is and why it matters—is critical to preserving it. At protests in the spring of 2025, Americans held signs that read DUE PROCESS and RULE OF LAW. It was a remarkable development in a country where, for so long, the common political wisdom was that Americans cared about kitchen table issues, not democracy itself. Understanding the importance of and the history behind the rule of law gives us the ability to have important conversations. If we are capable of articulating why the rule of law matters in these very concrete ways, we can help people who may not think any of this matters to them understand its importance. Want to be able to enter into business contracts with certainty your rights will be enforced, even if the people on the other side of them are well connected and wealthy? Then, "Hands off my rule of law!"

Democracy really does die in darkness, and it's our job to keep that from happening.

THE FOUNDING FATHERS' COMMON SENSE

You may have thought we'd already discussed the Founding Fathers as much as was profitable, but we're not done yet. They have a more direct link to modern political dangers than you might expect. In his 1949 novel *1984*, George Orwell wrote, "In a way, the world-view of the Party imposed itself most successfully on people incapable of understanding it. They could be made to accept the most flagrant violations of reality, because they never fully grasped the enormity of what was demanded of them, and were not sufficiently interested in public events to notice what was happening. By lack of understanding they remained sane. They simply swallowed everything." It is just what the Founding Fathers feared.

Like Orwell's *1984*, Margaret Atwood's *The Handmaid's Tale*, a 1985 dystopian novel about a totalitarian regime that controls women's bodies, foreshadowed the direction our politics have taken in an uncanny if (at least for now) exaggerated way, decades before it happened. Atwood has said she stopped writing *The Handmaid's Tale*, repeatedly, because it seemed "too far-fetched." The people in her fictional Gilead slipped readily into a theocracy where women's finances, bodies, and even their lives and their children were ultimately not their own. It was all made possible by a small group claiming the changes were essential to combat a serious threat—declining fertility. Both Orwell, a British journalist who covered the rise of fascism in Europe, and Atwood, a Canadian feminist, understood viscerally that democracy was not something to be taken for granted.

The Founding Fathers understood the vulnerability of the new nation they'd created, although they wrote in the realm of facts and law, not fiction. They tried to create a system of government that could resist a slide, like the ones portrayed in *1984* and *The Handmaid's Tale*, from democracy into monarchy or autocracy at the hands of a powerful individual or group that rose to power and was determined to benefit themselves, not the country. That was why Madison wrote *Federalist* 10, a profound warning as well as an explanation of political theory. He set it up like this: "The friend of popular governments never finds himself so much alarmed for their character and fate, as when he contemplates their propensity to this dangerous vice."

The dangerous vice that concerned Madison was factions. A faction, as he defined it, was a group of people in the country, "united and actuated by some common impulse of passion, or of interest, adverse to the rights of other citizens, or the permanent and aggregate interests of the community." The concern was that factions would develop—which Madison correctly saw as inevitable in a large nation—and put their own interests ahead of the good of the country. His take was that factions would most likely develop where there was "unequal distribution of property." He understood that this dividing line split society into groups with profoundly different interests. He feared it would become a fault line that could fracture American society.

Madison believed it wasn't possible to remove the causes of factionalism. So, the new Constitution would need to constrain the ways a faction could accumulate and exert power over others. Because the Constitution proposed a republic, not a pure democracy, he believed the new nation could meet this challenge in a way no other form of government could.

In a pure, or direct, democracy, everyone votes and whatever the majority decides goes. If the majority votes that on Tuesdays, everyone must wear a pink dress and eat a hamburger with mustard but no tomato on it, then that's what happens. It's easy to see how pure democracy can lead to a tyranny of the majority, especially the type of factions Madison feared, with either the haves or the have-nots seizing control and protecting themselves at the expense of the others. Madison wrote that pure democracies were doomed to fail because people don't agree in all regards about "their possessions, their opinions, and their passions," and that these differences, which might be managed in a small community, would be exacerbated by the size of the new country. The linchpin of his argument was that if a country were a republic, with people governed through their elected representatives, being big would actually become an advantage.

Madison explained that the new Constitution would prevent a tyranny of the majority, the failure brought on by factionalism, because of two key distinctions between a pure democracy and the Republic they had created. First, the "delegation of the government . . . to a small number of citizens elected by the rest" and, second, the large size of this representative form of government, which would impede the development of factions. Madison understood concerns about individual representatives who might disregard the people's wishes but felt this system struck the best of all possible balances. He argued that a larger republic, with a variety of diverse interests and a greater number of citizens, would make it difficult for a single faction to seize control and dominate government. This was because the sheer size and diversity of the country would dilute the influence any single faction could bring to bear. The final piece of the puzzle was the creation of a system of federalism, where "the federal Constitution forms a happy combination," in balance with state and local governments. The "great and aggregate interests" of the people would be handled by the federal government at the national level, and "the local and particular" were to be referred to the states and their legislatures.

The founders were very intentional. One of the joys of reading their original words is to see them as human beings engaged in the same debates we still have today. How do we make government work for the people? How do we build a solid economy? What can we do to prevent corruption, ensure a rising tide can lift all boats, and, hopefully, continue to expand the promise of democracy to more people in every successive generation? We might surprise these men, were they to walk into Congress today, with just how far we've taken their original promise and who is included as a citizen in our democracy. But I have no doubt they'd be proud of us and would firmly oppose a would-be tyrant's efforts to break down the system they established. The founders fully appreciated the risks that Orwell and Atwood would later write about in the guise of fiction. The founders wrote explicitly about how they expected their republican form of government to minimize those risks, both an explanation and a cautionary tale.

Here's the hard part. It hasn't always worked the way the founders wanted it to. Americans haven't always heeded their warnings. We live in a time when their expectation that only people of integrity would hear the call to public service has been eroded. But Madison and his colleagues weren't naive when they set that expectation. They were creating a standard for what Americans could demand of their elected representatives just as much as they were laying out a prediction for how our politics would work. That means that when our elected officials fail in their obligation to serve their constituents, we don't sit back, grumble a little bit, and accept it. Failure requires us to return to the baseline of the Founding Fathers' expectations and insist that our representatives serve with the fidelity the Constitution requires of them. This applies to all of them: The president, members of Congress, and even judges, especially those on the Supreme Court.

In Madison's view in *Federalist 10*, elected representatives would be more likely to set aside "local prejudices and schemes of injustice" and to work for the good of all than representatives selected by other means. And a large republic with "a greater variety of parties" would act as security against the risk of any one faction being "able to outnumber and oppress the rest," especially one with "secret wishes" designed to benefit their "unjust and interested majority." This led him to conclude:

> The influence of factious leaders may kindle a flame within their particular States, but will be unable to spread a general conflagration through the other States. A religious sect may degenerate into a political faction in a part of the Confederacy; but the variety of sects dispersed over the entire face of it must secure the national councils against any danger from that source. A rage for paper money, for an abolition of debts, for an equal division of property, or for any other improper or wicked project, will be less apt to pervade the whole body of the Union than a particular member of it; in the same proportion as such a malady is more likely to taint a particular county or district, than an entire State.

In some ways, we have become lapsed republicans—not the political party of that name, but people who live in a republican form of government—because we no longer dwell on the vices of factionalism and use the tools the Constitution provides to prevent it. While much of the country drifted into taking democracy for granted or simply not caring about it, a faction crept in, seeking to distort democracy for its own benefit. *Federalist* 10's message is to stay on guard and be a country where democracy is treasured. One way to do that is by committing to civics education, which can happen informally as well as in the classroom. If you're reading this book, you're educating yourself and developing the ability to bring others along with you. If people really want to make America great again, then we would treat the Constitution like the living, breathing document it must be if we are going to remain the Republic that Madison and his colleagues envisioned.

THAT TAKES US BACK TO ORWELL AND *1984*: "IN THE END THE PARTY would announce that two and two made five, and you would have to believe it. It was inevitable that they should make that claim sooner or later: the logic of their position demanded it. Not merely the validity of experience, but the very existence of external reality, was tacitly denied by their philosophy. The heresy of heresies was common sense." The orthodoxy of a totalitarian regime requires that we abandon thinking for ourselves. The remedy to an attempted takeover by a would-be dictator is to do precisely that. We must think for ourselves instead of unquestioningly accepting others' views. We must stay informed. That's our most fundamental duty as Americans right now. Don't look away. And don't hope it won't happen if you close your eyes. Surround yourself with supportive people and educate yourself; prepare for the days ahead. When the people with a vested interest in breaking the system tell you it is already broken beyond repair, be skeptical. The damage to the architecture of our democracy can be repaired by people of purpose. That is the task ahead of us.

UNDERSTANDING THE ORIGINS OF THE CONSTITUTION IS ESSENTIAL to securing the future of the Republic. We'll talk about what a modern vision of civics education might look like in chapter 6. But we have a bit more to discuss before we get there.

In the second month of the second Trump administration, as Trump's intention to unwind the constitutional balance of power became increasingly clear, Senator Angus King, an Independent from Maine, spoke out in a floor speech. King returned to the framework established by the founders to warn that Trump's attempt to seize congressional powers was "grossly unconstitutional." When Trump tried to claim Congress's power of the purse for his own, refusing to allocate federal funds to programs Congress had allocated them to, Senator King didn't mince words. He called it "absolutely straight up unconstitutional." "It's illegal," King said.

His words bear careful reading:

The reason the framers designed our Constitution the way they did was that they were afraid of concentrated power. They had just fought a brutal eight-year war with a king. They didn't want a king. They wanted a constitutional republic, where power was divided between the Congress and the President and the courts, and we are collapsing that structure. And the structure wasn't there for fun. It wasn't, hey, we'll design this complicated system. It was there to protect our freedom. Because the people that wrote our Constitution understood human nature, and they understood a very important thousand-year-old principle—power corrupts, and absolute power corrupts absolutely.

King understood not only the vision of Madison and the rest of the Founding Fathers, he also saw into the not-too-distant future. His prediction: "The people cheering this on I fear, in a reasonably short period of time, are going to say where did this go? How did this happen? How did we make our president into a monarch? How did this happen?" He answered his own question, looking out on the floor of the Senate and admonishing his colleagues, "How it happened is we gave it up! James Madison thought we would fight for our power, but no. Right now we're just sitting back and watching it happen." He reserved his final criticism for his fellow senators who didn't want to acknowledge the constitutional crisis we were already in: "Many of my friends in this body say it will be hard, we don't want to buck the President, we'll let the courts take care of it. . . . That's a cop-out. It's our responsibility to protect the Constitution. That's what we swear to when we enter this body." Angus King is the kind of person Madison expected us to elect. We should demand more from our officials, especially those King accused of copping out. We can't let them get away with acting like there's nothing they can do. That would be a cop-out on our part.

I like to think that had they lived in the same era, Angus King would have been friends with Thomas Paine. Paine was an unlikely candidate to become a Founding Father. Born in England, where he flunked out of grammar school at the age of twelve, he has been described as "a dabbler at many things, a failure at all." But when he published *Common Sense* on January 10, 1776, he helped Americans understand what was possible if they took responsibility for their own fate. By the end of the American Revolution, half a million copies had been sold. An estimated one in five Americans owned a copy of the forty-seven-page pamphlet. With literacy rates lower than they are today, Paine's words were shared even further—*Common Sense* was quite literally shouted on street corners and read aloud in neighborhood pubs. "The Cause of America," Paine wrote, "is in a great measure, the cause of all mankind."

Paine gave the colonists confidence that if they broke with Britain, they could succeed and prevail. He told them that they had the "power to begin the world over again," and they did it. Success wasn't a foregone conclusion at the time, but Paine made people believe in themselves and in their new nation.

We are a country that shook off the chains of a foreign king who dictated the course of our lives. Having done that and created a rule of law nation that firmly limits the power of a president and demands the other branches of government fulfill their constitutional obligations, we have all the tools we need to begin the world over again now. We can unshackle our country from a leader who wants to undo the American experiment. To do that, we have to first believe in ourselves and the power of democracy again.

When Paine wrote in his December 1776 pamphlet, *The*

American Crisis, that "these are the times that try men's souls," the Continental army was retreating from battlefield defeats. It was a moment when people in the new nation were far from certain about where it would all end, and independence from Britain wasn't guaranteed. The very existence of the United States was in doubt. But Paine's courage proved to be contagious.

His words still ring true today. Times that try our souls. Times when we find out who we are. We already know who we are not—we are not people who give up. We don't cower in the face of an elected president who wants to assume for himself more power than the Constitution permits until he is as powerful as the kings the founders dreaded.

In *Common Sense,* Paine explained the weaknesses of kings like this:

> Men who look upon themselves born to reign, and others to obey, soon grow insolent; selected from the rest of mankind their minds are early poisoned by importance; and the world they act in differs so materially from the world at large, that they have but little opportunity of knowing its true interests, and when they succeed to the government are frequently the most ignorant and unfit of any throughout the dominions.

On February 19, 2025, Donald Trump announced on Truth Social, the social media platform he owns, that he had involved himself in a matter affecting congestion traffic pricing in New York City. He ended his post with these words: "LONG

LIVE THE KING!" The official White House account on X and Instagram shared Trump's proclamation, adding an AI-generated fake *Time* magazine cover depicting a smug Trump wearing a golden crown. As Paine wrote, "most ignorant and unfit." As Senator King told his colleagues, if that behavior continues unchallenged it won't be long before Americans are forced to ask how they ended up with a king—or worse.

Paine reasoned that "a long habit of not thinking a thing wrong, gives it a superficial appearance of being right, and raises at first a formidable outcry in defense of custom. But the tumult soon subsides. Time makes more converts than reason." That's where we are now. For those of us who have always held fast to our belief in democracy, the path is clear. Others, those who were so taken with the snake oil promises of greatness that they flirted with a path that diverged from democracy, may have a more difficult road back. A faction that uses cheap promises to convince people to forgo the stability offered by the rule of law can be appealing until, suddenly, it isn't.

Time will make converts and we will nudge that process along, because elections, the last bastion of democracy, are around the corner. We live in a different world from the one Paine inhabited. *Common Sense* was an argument to separate from Britain. But what rings loudly across the centuries is the fact that we must determine our own futures—and that we can. We don't need a king. Paine believed British rule was the cause of most of the problems of the day and that independence was the solution. Today, independence from tyranny is still the solution. Same song. New verse. But we can still do this.

The American Crisis begins with the famous words, "These are the times that try men's souls." Paine's next lines are less often quoted but no less valuable: "The summer soldier and the sunshine patriot will, in this crisis, shrink from the service of their country; but he that stands it now, deserves the love and thanks of man and woman. Tyranny, like hell, is not easily conquered." His conclusion to that essay still holds an important message for us, almost as though this were still 1776. "There are persons, too, who see not the full extent of the evil which threatens them; they solace themselves with hopes that the enemy, if he succeed, will be merciful. It is the madness of folly, to expect mercy from those who have refused to do justice."

It is indeed madness. Democracy or nothing.

HOW DO WE KNOW FROM OUR HISTORY THAT AMERICANS CAN SUCceed in the face of factions developing in our population and our government who would destroy our freedoms? We know because we've already done it.

In the 1950s, under McCarthyism and the "Red Scare," people were afraid to push back against the bully, Senator Joseph McCarthy, whose aggressive and frequently baseless accusations against people he didn't like ruined lives in government, entertainment, and academia. McCarthy called people communist traitors despite the absence of any evidence that they were either. He used public hearings and fear to consolidate power.

For a time, people didn't stand up. They were afraid of being labeled communists themselves if they did. The media, for the most part, repeated McCarthy's claims, and very few politicians of the day were willing to challenge his tactics, thinking only of self-preservation. Even President Dwight D. Eisenhower avoided confrontation with him until the end.

McCarthy destroyed careers. Had he been given free rein for much longer, he would have destroyed the First Amendment too. He damaged it deeply while he remained in power. An atmosphere of fear prevailed in America. McCarthy's power grew because of silence and self-preservation. It only came to an end when others finally said "enough." It didn't take an army or a rebellion. It took American common sense and persistence.

Early in 1954, McCarthy asked for preferential treatment for an aide on his subcommittee who was drafted. Apparently unhappy with how the situation was handled, McCarthy decided to go after the army with an allegation that security at a top secret facility was inadequate. There were three months of nationally televised hearings.

Senate records tell the story of how it ended: "The army hired Boston lawyer Joseph Welch to make its case. At a session on June 9, 1954, McCarthy charged that one of Welch's attorneys had ties to a Communist organization. As an amazed television audience looked on, Welch responded with the immortal lines that ultimately ended McCarthy's career: 'Until this moment, Senator, I think I never really gauged your cruelty or your recklessness.' When McCarthy tried to continue his attack, Welch angrily interrupted, 'Let us not assassinate this lad further, senator. You have done enough. Have you no sense of decency?'"

Suddenly, it was over. Seemingly overnight, McCarthy's hold on the country began to dissipate. His Senate colleagues and his party abandoned him; the media stopped parroting his accusations. Three years later, he was dead.

Americans don't have to give in to the bully. As with McCarthy, sometimes it just takes one courageous moment to show the public a tyrant's absurdity, his malice, and to consign him to history as a second lost cause in the American story. With bullies, people have often had enough long before they are ready to admit it. With an arbitrary tyrant, they are often afraid to. Maybe we are headed for a public moment like the one that felled Senator McCarthy. Whether or not we are, the ultimate way to challenge the bully is at the ballot box. In 2026, every seat in the House of Representatives will be on the ballot, as will thirty-three seats in the Senate. If you want to ask Trump "Have you no sense of decency?" make him face Democratic majorities in both bodies of Congress.

CHAPTER 5

RBG's Umbrella

You've undoubtedly heard a politician or two say, "This next election will be the most important one of your life." You may have rolled your eyes and sighed a little, even if you care deeply about our democracy, because you've heard it so many times. Still, I hope this book has made the case that it's true: The next election is always the most important one of our lives. If you're concerned about the erosion of democratic norms and institutions, the way back is through the vote.

Will there *be* a next election in the United States? This is one of the questions I'm asked most frequently. Newly minted autocrats—especially those who rise to power in free and fair elections—like to cloak themselves in the semblance of legitimacy that holding elections offers. It's what Hungary's Prime

Minister Viktor Orbán has done through four consecutive election cycles, continuing elections but putting his thumb on the scale in his own favor in what he openly acknowledges as the "illiberal democracy" he has created in that country. Even Vladimir Putin permits elections to be held in Russia. He won his fifth in 2024, albeit with no meaningful opposition. Putin's opponents are all dead or imprisoned.

If an American president tried to stop elections entirely, the public outcry would be swift. As a practical matter, we hold fifty state elections (plus some in territories and others for military and overseas voters), not a national one, so it would be difficult to exercise some sort of top-down control to halt them. If you have to vote in person, like I do in Alabama, you know that, regardless of party politics, poll workers are fiercely protective of their precinct and their process, often in a way that defies partisanship.

So, the better question is: Will the next elections be free and fair? And what can we do to make sure that they are? The courts have gradually eroded the protections of the Voting Rights Act, leaving less room for private plaintiffs—like the civil rights groups that have traditionally stepped in to litigate when Americans' voting rights come under attack—to sue. Instead, the courts have interpreted the act to mean that only the Justice Department can sue in many situations. Of course, in its current incarnation, the Justice Department is eschewing that role.

If you want to know how to save the Republic, the answer is, do everything you can to protect the right to vote. And also, although this would seem to go without saying, make sure that *you* vote. We can all educate ourselves about the candidates, not just the national ones at the top of the ticket, but also mayors, state court judges, and members of the legislature and local school boards. It takes a little time, but every single one of those elections matters. The local ones, in particular, can have a tremendous impact on our daily lives and are frequently decided by small margins. Treat elections and your preparation for them with the seriousness you would a major exam that holds the key to your future, because they do.

THE MAN WHO CARED ABOUT VOTING

The right to vote is precious, almost sacred. It is the most powerful nonviolent tool or instrument in a democratic society. We must use it.

—John Lewis

Because voting, and helping other people vote, is deeply personal to me, I want to share a story with you. It was the last weekend in February 2020. I was in Selma, Alabama, for Jubilee, the annual commemoration of the march across the Edmund Pettus Bridge, which I've written about in chapter 3— the march that was led by John Lewis. For a half century, people from across the nation have made the pilgrimage to Selma to mark this day—civil rights activists, people of faith, students of history, and politicians, including, especially in election years, presidential candidates and sitting presidents.

In February of that year, the Covid lockdowns had not

yet begun, although the threat of something unpredictable loomed. There was real tension in the air even though the day was bright and sunny and old friends were gathered together. I was visiting with former colleagues as I prepared to speak on a panel in Selma's historic Brown Chapel, the same church the marchers had started out from all those years ago. The panel topic was state laws that prevented people with old felony convictions from voting and how their rights could (and should) be restored after they had served their sentences. The moderator was one of the finest lawyers I know, the Legal Defense Fund's Leah Aden, a leading civil rights litigator who would go on to argue *Alexander v. South Carolina State Conference of the NAACP*, the South Carolina redistricting case, before the US Supreme Court in 2023.

The panel discussion and the questions that followed were provocative, and the company was uplifting. It felt, in a way, as if we could already touch a future where we would move beyond the constant turmoil of Donald Trump's time in office and get back to work on the important priorities, like criminal justice reform and voting rights, that animated so many of our professional lives.

If you care about democracy and civil rights, visiting Selma will recharge your batteries. It does that even in good years, when progress is being made. You feel a rekindled commitment to do the right thing. There is nothing quite like being there, on sacred ground, and feeling deep in your bones what people were willing to sacrifice in the name of being part of our democracy. That's in a good year. In 2020, being there, being surrounded by decent, committed people, felt positively essential to carrying on.

After the panel, I walked out of the packed crowd in Brown Chapel, deep in thought, when a young woman approached me to ask if I could speak with her uncle. His name was George Sallie, and he was one of the original foot soldiers who faced Alabama state troopers at the bridge march in 1965. He was now in his nineties.

George Sallie had a problem. He had voted in every election since it became possible for him to register. But now, with the Alabama Democratic primary just days away on March 3, he'd been told he wouldn't be able to vote. Mr. Sallie didn't have a driver's license or a passport. There were a few other items the new Alabama Voter ID law would have let him use to establish his identity, like a student or military ID, but this man was in his nineties; he didn't have any of them either. Alabama's secretary of state had made a lot of noise about the availability of free state-issued IDs, but in rural Dallas County down in Alabama's Black Belt, Mr. Sallie hadn't been able to obtain one.

Alabama Republicans had justified their new Voter ID Act, while it was working its way through the state legislature, as a way of preventing voter fraud. But now, a man who had fought for the right of *all* Alabamians to vote was being denied that very right because he didn't have, and really couldn't get, the required kind of identification. Like so many measures that allegedly crack down on voter fraud, this law had the effect of suppressing voting rights. It was about to keep George Sallie from voting.

We enlisted a young lawyer to help. She was in Selma for Jubilee and was able to stay and accompany Mr. Sallie to the polls to make sure he could take advantage of a provision in the law that hadn't been widely publicized but that permitted a poll worker who knew him to vouch for his identity. It was a fortunate confluence of circumstances—a well-informed lawyer willing to help and a poll worker who could vouch for Mr. Sallie's identity.

Not every American who encounters difficulties voting is fortunate enough to have a lawyer at their side. And since 2020, even more restrictions have been imposed that make it more difficult for eligible Americans to vote. Disenfranchisement can be as simple as not being notified of a change in the location of your precinct or as complicated as George Sallie's situation. A bill circulating on Capitol Hill and an executive order being challenged in the courts would both require people to prove they are citizens before they can register to vote or update their registration, which would mean even fewer forms of identification would suffice. Some states are considering more restrictive measures too. But there are good people across the country, from politicians to poll workers, who are committed to making sure our elections work. What we need in this country now, more than ever, is to make sure that Americans with experience in different phases of the electoral process are connected so that people who can help are in touch with those who, like Mr. Sallie, need it to be able to vote.

In an interview with a local newspaper decades after it happened, George Sallie described being "hit upside the head" on Bloody Sunday. When he spoke about how he and other marchers were beaten and sprayed with tear gas by Alabama state troopers, you saw in his face that it was still real for him. When Mr. Sallie told you that he voted in every election as soon as he was able to register after the events in Selma, you knew it for the truth.

George Sallie passed away in 2024. And his legacy is helping us understand the power of the vote. It's more than the ability to decide who represents us, as important as that is. When we vote, we belong to democracy, and democracy to us.

VOTER FRAUD OR VOTER SUPPRESSION?

We do not have government by the majority. We have government by the majority who participate.

—often attributed to Thomas Jefferson, likely incorrectly

Congress passed the Voting Rights Act in the summer of 1965, and President Lyndon Johnson signed it into law on August 6 of that year. The Act was passed in large part as a result of the marches in Selma and the public response to them. The law required Congress to periodically reauthorize portions of the act, and it did that on a bipartisan basis, also expanding its protections, in 1970, 1975, 1982, and 2006—all years when a Republican occupied the White House. When he signed the 2006 reauthorization, President George W. Bush said, "The Voting Rights Act of 1965 (VRA) was designed to restore the birthright of every American—the right to choose our leaders. It has been vital to guaranteeing the right to vote for generations of Americans and has helped millions of our citizens enjoy the full promise of freedom." The reauthorization Bush signed in 2006 was supposed to extend the Voting Rights Act for another twenty-five years.

But then Shelby County, Alabama—just south of Birmingham—challenged the constitutionality of one of the most important provisions of the act, Section 5, in 2010, and won in the US Supreme Court in 2013. Before the Court decided *Shelby County v. Holder*, the Voting Rights Act required areas of the country where there was a history of discrimination—some entire states and parts of others—to submit new laws or changes in their election administration for "preclearance" before they could go into effect. Preclearance requests had to be submitted to either the attorney general or the district court in the District of Columbia, for a determination that the change would not perpetuate discrimination against racial, ethnic, or language minorities.

In his majority opinion in *Shelby County*, Chief Justice John Roberts invalidated the coverage formula that was used to decide which jurisdictions had to submit to preclearance before they could implement changes to voting. He opined that great progress in matters of race had been made.

The decision effectively ended preclearance. In the absence of any valid criteria for deciding which jurisdictions had to submit to preclearance, none of them were required to comply with the requirement any longer. The opinion invited Congress to update the law with fresh information, so new criteria could be established. Despite the earlier bipartisan reverence for voting rights, that never happened. In some ways, the hyper-political divide in our country dates back to the decision in Shelby County, and the subsequent revelation that Congressional Republicans had no intention of restoring Section 5 of the Voting Rights Act.

Suddenly, it was the Wild West when it came to voting. States could implement all sorts of strange restrictions purportedly designed to stop voter fraud, which in fact were little more than intentional measures to suppress the rights of lawful voters. It was in the days following the *Shelby County* decision that Alabama's Voter ID law, the one that almost kept George Sallie from voting, quietly moved into effect, without review by either the Justice Department or the Court. The state had passed it and relied on *Shelby County* to permit it to put the new law into effect without ever submitting it for preclearance, which it likely couldn't have passed.

Justice Ruth Bader Ginsburg dissented from the majority's decision in *Shelby County*. She wrote, with prescient clarity, that ending preclearance was "like throwing away your umbrella in a rainstorm because you are not getting wet." Everything the Court has done since then, to thin out protections for voting rights, has proved her right. Taking down the umbrella didn't make sense when the chief justice wrote the majority opinion, and it doesn't make sense now. It was a fundamental betrayal of the American people, especially in tandem with the Court's 2010 decision in *Citizens United v. Federal Election Commission*, the decision that did away with campaign finance restrictions, making it possible for corporations and other groups to inject "dark money" into politics—large sums whose origins aren't made public when donated through super PACs. Americans no longer knew which interests were backing certain candidates, and it could be increasingly difficult to vote against them in any event.

As Americans, we should be concerned about our neighbors' right to vote as much as our own. The fundamental premise of this great nation—that we aren't ruled by kings but instead by fellow citizens we select—must be secured and protected by each generation. Politicians often bemoan low turnout numbers and blame voters, when they should, in fact, be finding solutions that make it easier for people to vote. If they won't do it, and they haven't, then it's up to us.

There is a still more extreme form of voter suppression, one that is even more insidious that we need to confront. It involves trying to convince people that their vote doesn't matter, so they shouldn't bother with voting. Cases like *Shelby County* and *Citizens United*, efforts to strip us of the right to vote, are offered by people who would keep us from voting as reasons we shouldn't even try. This seductive argument suggests that certain people, the people those telling the story don't want to vote, should just give up.

The reality is, people who know your vote really does make a difference want you to stay home if they think you won't vote for them. If anything underscores the importance of voting, it's how hard some people will fight to keep you from casting a ballot and to keep your ballot from being counted. We shape our politics by participating—in everything from voting for local sheriffs who determine law enforcement priorities in our communities to choosing presidents who select Supreme Court justices. Your vote matters—and anyone who tells you it doesn't has an agenda. Ask yourself what it is.

LAWS LIKE THE VOTING RIGHTS ACT OF 1965 THAT PROHIBIT RACIAL discrimination and judges like Frank Johnson in Montgomery, Alabama, who enforced them made it easier to exercise the right to vote. So, forces that wanted to prevent Black citizens from voting turned to new tactics. Chief among them was manufacturing a rampant fear of voter fraud, despite a total absence of evidence establishing it existed, let alone impacted election outcomes. Republican politicians used it to claim restrictive measures were necessary to keep people who weren't eligible to vote from voting, and to keep people who were qualified to vote from voting more than once. New rules were designed or applied in ways that made it more difficult for "people" to vote. I put "people" in quotation marks, because let's be real: These rules were aimed not at all people but at a few groups in particular, especially Black voters. Although some date the voter fraud narrative to this century, it was at work in the Deep South much earlier. Voter fraud is a bogeyman born out of the desire to suppress Black voters from exercising their rights.

How concerned should we be about voter fraud? Studies have repeatedly shown it to be vanishingly rare. A 2012 data collection study suggested enhanced identification for voting was unnecessary because it found fewer than ten cases of voter impersonation nationwide between 2000 and 2012. Law professor Justin Levitt, who went on to head the Voting

Rights Section of the Justice Department's Civil Rights Division during the Obama administration, reported in August 2014 that he found only thirty-one credible claims of voter impersonation out of one billion ballots cast between 2000 and 2014. In other words, roughly one out of every thirty million ballots. Levitt has been chronicling allegations of fraud for more than two decades. The data confirm it is very rare and certainly not the type of problem that would justify mass intrusion on the right to vote. Somehow, though, a narrative made it into circulation long before Donald Trump emerged on our political scene that asserted significant voter fraud was taking place and insinuated that Democrats were responsible, so measures to control *them* were both necessary and acceptable.

These stories are easy to spread, but claims that fraud impacts the outcome of our elections remain unproven. That's because it's a myth. And as we saw in the wake of the 2020 election, the real fraud that is going on here is more likely the fraudulent *claims* of voter fraud. While there is no evidence that any of the measures Republicans have suggested, like identification requirements or curtailing absentee and mail-in voting, would solve this theoretical fraud problem, even if it existed, there is the very real problem that these unnecessary measures disenfranchise citizens who are eligible to vote.

Over time, these myths, like the ones claiming that there is a noncitizen waiting to vote around every corner and that people are being bused from one state to another to cast multiple ballots, have taken root in our country. But study after study confirms that fraud is not impacting the outcome of our elections. Donald Trump did not come up with the idea of using unwarranted fears of election fraud as a way to suppress the vote. It was deeply entrenched long before he formally entered the political arena in 2016. Trump simply took it to new and extreme heights, including using it as an excuse for losing an election.

A functional democracy requires an engaged citizenry. And that means voters. But too many Americans don't vote. According to Pew Research Center, more Americans voted in 2018, 2020, and 2022 than the number who had voted in elections for decades. But even then, 34 percent of eligible voters stayed home for the 2020 presidential election, and in the 2018 midterms, 51 percent of Americans didn't vote, although that election saw the highest turnout for a midterm since 1914. Approximately 36 percent didn't cast a ballot in 2024.

Generations after Selma, many Americans, from different walks of life and for a wide range of reasons, still don't vote. Some simply aren't interested. Others don't vote because it's inconvenient, especially for those who work, live in rural areas, have fewer resources, and so on. The dearth of early voting days, absentee voting, and vote-by-mail are all contributing factors. And other voters have been told, and have come to believe, that their vote doesn't make a difference.

Why is there so much resistance to making it easy for eligible Americans to vote? Why shouldn't it be as simple as a family sitting together around their kitchen table as they fill in their mail-in ballots? Why shouldn't registration be automatic? If we're worried about fraudulent registrations, why not develop better training for workers involved in that process instead of overcompensating and denying Americans their most fundamental right?

Keep reminding yourself: People wouldn't work so hard to interfere with the right to vote if it didn't matter so much. So have confidence and vote. Remind the people around you that if they sit out an election because they don't think their vote matters or they think you can teach someone a lesson by withholding it, or just because it's too much trouble to wait in the increasingly long lines some voters are faced with, they're siding with the people who don't want them to vote. Have the courage of George Sallie, and make sure you vote in every single election.

Voting allows us to alter the course of history. You are more than just one vote. You are part of a powerful body politic that has the right to decide who will lead us. If the Trump administration and its allies in some states try to make it harder for us to vote in the next election, we'll find a way. Don't give up! No matter what happens, no matter how unfair it may be, our job is to work together to make sure people can register to vote, stay registered, vote, and have their votes count.

Those are the four essential steps in the process. Let's consider each one in turn.

REGISTERING

It should be easy for eligible Americans to register to vote. Federal law says you can do it online. The National Voter

Registration Act (often called the Motor Voter Act) requires states to let people who are getting a driver's license, registering a new boat, and so on register to vote in federal elections on the same form they complete for their vehicles and licenses. The law also lets people register to vote when they sign up for public assistance or other state-funded programs. The idea is to remove the barriers to registration.

But some people want to resurrect those barriers. In 2016, Alabama Secretary of State John Merrill gave an interview where he said, "As long as I'm secretary of state of Alabama, you're going to have to show some initiative to become a registered voter in this state." He referred to voting as a "privilege."

That's incorrect. Voting is a right, not a privilege. If you're an American citizen, you're entitled to do it. Making you jump through hoops to register or to stay registered is the kind of cowardice engaged in by people who don't think they can earn your vote.

While this book was in progress, two such proposals were circulating. The first was the Safeguard American Voter Eligibility (SAVE) Act. The second was an executive order ironically titled "Preserving and Protecting the Integrity of American Elections," signed by Donald Trump. Both wanted to force people to provide proof of citizenship before they could register to vote and every time they updated their registration, for instance, for a change of address. It doesn't sound that bad at first. We all know that only citizens are eligible to vote, so why not? Then you stop to think. What do you have on hand that proves you're an American citizen? A passport—they're expensive, but if you happen to have an unexpired one, it will do the trick. A birth certificate or some kinds of military ID will also work. But at least twenty-one million Americans don't have proof readily available. Only 51 percent of Americans have passports, which cost $165, plus additional money to assemble the documents you need, get a photograph of yourself, and travel to your appointment location. The new Trump administration measures could end voter registration by mail and online because voters would have to show proof of citizenship to election officials "in person" when they register. That would also make it difficult, if not impossible, to conduct voter registration drives at churches or schools. States that automatically register voters when they turn eighteen would no longer be able to do so. And if you move or need to reregister for any reason, these rules would apply to you. You'd have to bring your passport or birth certificate in for inspection every single time.

There are better ways to guarantee registrants are citizens without making it this difficult for people to register. States have employees who are trained to run checks after forms are completed, before registrants are added to voter rolls. And, of course, it's a crime for a noncitizen to vote in a federal election. It's hard to believe significant numbers of people would go to the trouble it takes to come to this country without legal immigration status, start a new life in the shadows, and then offer themselves up for prosecution and deportation by voting illegally.

When this book went to print, the future of the SAVE Act and Trump's executive order on voting were uncertain. Some states had similar measures under consideration, in case the federal ones didn't survive. It's a good time to make sure you have the right ID to register and vote with, in case these measures are the law of the land next time we go to the polls.

STAYING REGISTERED

Registering is not enough. Americans have to worry about staying registered too. Some voters have had the experience of going to the polls, confident they were registered, only to discover they'd been "pruned" from the voter rolls, moved to inactive status. Some states send postcards to voters who haven't shown up for a few elections, asking them to return the card if they want to remain registered. Of course, so many things could go wrong there—everything from a misdelivered card to a voter who chucks it because it looks like junk mail.

Unfortunately, these techniques are now a fact of life. There are better ways to keep the voter rolls up to date than assuming everyone who doesn't return a postcard, which they may not have even received, no longer wants to be a registered voter. But the Supreme Court has approved these voter roll pruning measures. It authorized their use in a 2018 Ohio case, *Husted v. A. Philip Randolph Institute*. Justice Samuel Alito wrote the majority opinion and was joined by Chief Justice John Roberts and Justices Anthony Kennedy, Clarence Thomas, and Neil Gorsuch. At the time *Husted* was decided, a number of other states used some form of this approach to remove voters from the rolls too. The decision greenlit their practices along with Ohio's. Using postcards as a gatekeeping device to determine who gets removed from voter rolls doesn't line up with the importance of the right to vote. This approach might pass muster to determine who wants to renew their season football tickets, but it shouldn't suffice for a fundamental right.

There's nothing nefarious in the basic idea of keeping voter rolls current—they should be updated to reflect people who have passed away or moved. But it should be done in a way that doesn't disenfranchise eligible citizens. Proponents of these measures say that voters who are removed from the rolls can still cast a provisional ballot. But for that provisional ballot to be counted, the voter must make an additional trip, sometimes to a different location, by a certain date, with all their identification. For a voter who doesn't get paid time off from work for voting, or who must watch family during the hours government offices are open, this can be an insurmountable burden.

Each state has its own rules for voting, so there is some variation among the states that use the process *Husted* authorized. But pruning voter rolls in this cavalier fashion makes it more difficult for voters to stay registered everywhere it's done. The government can't treat your First Amendment right to free speech or your Second Amendment right to possess firearms as a privilege—you possess those rights, and they cannot be violated. Voting shouldn't be burdened more than other rights, but that's what's happening.

There's a step you can take ahead of federal elections to make sure you stay on the active voter rolls. And it's easy. You can go online and check your registration status. Most states have a website, and many have their own apps. If yours doesn't, sites like Vote.org or IWillVote.com let voters nationwide check their status. And here's the best part: The Motor Voter Act says you can't be removed from the voter rolls less than ninety days before an election. So, if you check your status on day eighty-nine and you're an active voter, your eligibility can't change before the election. Take a screenshot, keep it handy, and if there are any issues, you've got proof that you are an active voter. Make sure everyone in your circle does it too!

Getting registered is only the first step. It's equally important to make sure you stay registered. Now you know how to do it.

VOTING

In the early 2000s, now-Senator Angus King and former professional wrestler Jesse Ventura were governors of their respective states of Maine and Minnesota. They had a running bet over which state would have the highest voter turnout in elections. Not surprisingly, the two were usually neck and neck for the best turnout rates in the country. Pro-democracy leaders want *everyone* who is eligible to vote, and they are willing to do the work to convince voters to pick them, instead of trying to pick their voters.

Governors King and Ventura understood something important. Who you vote for is a political choice. But making sure people *can* vote is an essential right, and every elected official is obligated, if they take their oath of office seriously, to do whatever they can to make it possible for Americans to exercise it. The act of voting is fundamentally American, a quintessential right of citizenship. Guaranteeing the right to vote is about democracy, not politics, and the only kind of people who belong in office in our country are people who understand and honor that.

Voting can get complicated. Each jurisdiction has its own rules and ballots. It's a process that works because thousands of committed election officials and poll workers across the country make it happen. Each state has its own election rules, and because they can change, it's important to stay up to date. Find your secretary of state's website and put it to use. Other pro-voting organizations have this information on their websites too. Figure out whom you can trust and arm yourself with information about whether your state has early voting or not, what hours your polls are open, where your precinct is, what ID you will need to vote, and so forth. Be ready to vote.

Sometimes, all it takes for an uncertain voter to make the decision to participate is a little bit of encouragement, some direction to help them figure out how they can make informed choices. Make plans with friends and family to vote together or meet afterward. And be alert to help people who may need assistance to vote, like the elderly neighbor who needs a ride to the polls and help with the line, or young parents who have to get kids to school and themselves to work and could use your support. If it becomes more difficult to vote, then let's all go out of our way, each doing whatever we can and taking whatever help we need to make voting possible. That wise woman who told us it takes a village really was right.

Our pandemic experience proved that we can have secure elections while using techniques that make voting more accessible, like mail-in and absentee ballots, early voting days, same-day registration, and more. States with strong pro-voting cultures, like Maine and Minnesota, encourage Americans to educate themselves about candidates and vote. If you're lucky enough to live in one of these states, you can become part of that culture and find a way to advance it. If you aren't, you can be part of developing a powerful citizen advocacy plan and moving your state, or your neighborhood, forward.

Jayla Allen was a few years out of college when I had the privilege of speaking with her. She went to Prairie View A&M, one of the nation's historically Black colleges and universities. Prairie View is in Waller County, Texas, where the political leadership is predominantly white. Students and other Black citizens in the county have experienced extreme voter suppression efforts. Allen followed in the footsteps of other family members when she went off to Prairie View. Part of what she learned in college was how to be a voting rights activist in a place where Black people often had to struggle to exercise their right to vote.

One of the biggest insights Allen shared with me was that it was often local elections, not national ones, that activated younger voters. Those races give them a clear opportunity to see how they can exert influence over the issues that matter most in their daily lives, like local taxes or parking ticket collection policies. They might not ever meet a US president or a senator—but they could have real access to help shape the policies of a small-town mayor or sheriff. "It's mind-blowing," she told me. "It shows you the power you have."

Then she told me a story. A mom reached out to her on Facebook, saying her daughter was a student at Prairie View and newly eligible to vote. She asked Allen to help her daughter register and take her to the polls. Allen did. She walked the young woman through the entire process, making it easier for her to vote. She told me it was an honor she would never forget. "That's why I'll always do the work," she said.

So, vote. But take someone along with you. Maybe a first-time voter. Maybe someone who needs a little help. Voting is about being part of a community.

MAKING SURE YOUR VOTE GETS COUNTED

As a deputy voter registrar in Waller County, Allen helped more than five hundred residents register and vote. But not every ballot that gets cast gets counted. The final step in the process is following through. It's not enough to vote; you also have to make sure that your ballot gets counted—literally. Today, many states have online portals or apps that can be used to make sure a mail-in ballot reaches its destination. In states with rigorous rules for signature matches or rigid requirements involving multiple envelopes, it's especially important to follow up to ensure there are no technical flaws that prevent a ballot from being counted. After you vote, make sure you follow through, using whatever mechanism your state has in place, to ensure your ballot gets counted. If there's a holdup, do whatever it takes to ensure your vote gets counted, not canceled out. It's easy to overlook this final step, and it shouldn't require this level of diligence to exercise a right. But in this environment, we have to evolve and be smarter voters who protect our own rights.

WHAT CAN WE DO?

Don't let voting rights be just one more issue in an era of political overload. Voting is *the* issue. Talk with your friends, family, and colleagues about voting and help them understand why it's singularly important. We often undervalue these one-on-one conversations, but ultimately, you're the person the people around you trust the most. The best place to start is to encourage people to register. That sets them on the path to voting. Have confidence in your ability to explain and persuade them. And if words aren't your strong suit, you can give them this book.

The number of Americans who are actively interested in elections has increased in the current political climate. But even with that, almost 90 million of the 245 million Americans who were eligible to vote in 2024 didn't. If you want to save democracy, persuade potential voters who don't vote, or don't vote regularly, that their participation is essential. Many Americans are intermittent voters who vote only some of the time. Among voters who were eligible to vote in national elections in 2018, 2020, and 2022, 70 percent voted in at least one, but only 37 percent voted in all of them. Registration is the starting point, but don't stop there. Make plans to vote together.

The question of why younger people don't vote in robust numbers is particularly pressing. Statistics in election after election show low voter participation among those between ages eighteen and twenty-nine. In the 2022 midterm elections, youth turnout ranged from just 13 percent of those who were eligible to 37 percent in states where it was easier to register and vote. Younger voters have enormous opportunities to shape their communities, their states, and the country by voting consistently and supporting candidates who represent their priorities. So how do we help them develop a stronger pro-voting culture?

It's easy to pin our hopes on a magic bullet, a big, bold gesture from a Beyoncé or a Taylor Swift who gets fans excited about registering and voting. And that can help. But what it really takes is more personal. We need to all be involved, even if that means bringing just one more person into the active electorate. You're more likely to attend a movie or a lecture or a party if a friend invites you to go along with them. The same is true for voting. Success comes from Americans encouraging other Americans to vote, especially new voters and young voters who might need that invitation to get started. Vote and make it as easy as possible for the people around you to vote. Encourage friends to vote like their future depends upon it—because it does.

Prior to her last speech before stepping down, I had the honor of introducing then–Attorney General Loretta Lynch when she reminded the congregation at Sixteenth Street

Baptist Church in Birmingham, Alabama, that the most important role any of us can have in this country is that of private citizen and voter. Imagine our country if we all took responsibility for turning out the vote. There are a lot of options. For starters, you can volunteer to work the polls, help with voter education programs, be a poll watcher, drive people to the polls, or help people get identification. We need to create a culture where there is FOMO—fear of missing out— for people who don't vote. Today there is no expectation that everyone will vote. Our challenge is to create one.

Some Americans have had the good fortune of growing up in civically engaged homes. Voting comes naturally for them. For those who haven't been raised in that environment or those who need encouragement or support voting for any reason, don't be afraid to hold their hands and help them vote. Courage—and voting—are contagious.

In *Shelby County v. Holder*, Justice Ginsburg took the majority to task for failing to honor the long-standing tradition of protecting the right to vote. In her dissenting opinion, she quoted Dr. Martin Luther King Jr., and when she read her dissent from the bench that day in 2013, she added a crucial point of emphasis: "The arc of the moral universe is long, but it bends toward justice *if there is a steadfast commitment to see the task through to completion.*" Our job is to keep Justice Ginsburg's umbrella open and make sure it protects everyone from those who would take away their right to vote.

CHAPTER 6

We Are the Cavalry

We no longer live in a world that requires a storm-the-palace coup for a dictator to take over a democracy. A would-be autocrat can come into power by commandeering key institutions after winning an election, cloaked in an aura of legality. He can use disinformation to mislead. He can play on a general lack of interest in government to convince a country that he's in the process of delivering what it voted for. He can maintain a pretense of democracy. He can lie and promise free and fair elections in the future. He can use the institutions to target his personal enemies—anyone who would oppose him—threatening them with criminal prosecution and civil actions, claiming they are the ones who are violating the rule of law. He can use tax audits or withhold permission for business deals as a form of punishment. He can target opposition leaders' livelihoods as a lesson to every-one else. He can defund schools and organizations that en-courage people to think freely. A competent bureaucracy can be replaced with a kleptocracy (government by the corrupt) and a kakistocracy (government in the hands of the grossly incompetent). He can rewrite history to glorify himself. And before you know it, that's the ball game. The country is a nominal democracy, a republic in name only.

Who is going to fight back? Who *is* fighting back?

Congress? Politicians? Lawyers? Some will. Civil society groups will rally to their causes. But here's the reality: The cavalry isn't coming. The courts aren't the cavalry, and there will be no politician swooping in to save us. There are good people in both places who are doing their best, but ultimately, they need our help as much as we need theirs. It's us. We're the cavalry.

Although we may be *on our own*, we are *not all alone*. We truly are in this together. We have one another, a community of like-minded people across the country who care about de-mocracy. That may seem to be a slender thread, but it's how we, like others who have faced similar challenges in the past, are going to get through this.

So, gather your resources and take courage. Yes, Donald Trump has undeniably turned away from democratic princi-ples and put the country on the path toward authoritarian-ism. The Supreme Court has inexplicably played along in key moments. But the fact that you start down a road doesn't mean your final destination is inevitable. We live in unpre-dictable times. Guardrails could suddenly reemerge in the form of people with character and conscience or a reconfiguration of congressional majorities. The combined opposition from the people, the courts, and some members of Congress may suddenly create that moment of national consensus we've been struggling to find. But it's more likely that we are in this fight for democracy for the long haul. It won't be a straight line forward, so we'd better get ready to face it with grace, style, humor, and one another. We can't let the fight for democracy become drudgery; we have to prepare ourselves for it joyfully without taking it any less seriously. It's a plan for the worst and hope for the best kind of moment.

The most important piece of knowledge to carry with you is that you are not powerless. That's a myth, constructed by the very same people who understand that an autocrat's biggest vulnerability is a well-informed, engaged citizenry. Nobel laureate Aleksandr Solzhenitsyn, who fought back against Soviet oppression by exposing it, wrote, "The simple step of a courageous man is not to take part in the lie." It's a sobering thought and no small thing, but it's something we can all try to do. It requires bravery, and we will summon it together.

How do we pull together what we know about fighting for democracy so that we are equipped to preserve it? What is the common thread between what we know, what we need our fellow citizens to know, and what we can do? How do we encourage as many Americans as possible to participate in politics and elections? How do we keep democracy safe in this moment when it is fragile and in danger, and do it in a way that makes the investment and the interest and the commitment last longer than just right now, so the country doesn't find itself in this position again a stone's throw down the road? We have to ask the right questions, the ones I've just mentioned and more, to get to the right answers.

Democracy, by its nature and by the design of the Founding Fathers, requires that its citizens participate in the process. To do that, you have to understand it. That means reinvigorating civics education because we have a real deficit in that area that calls for updating both how we think about it and how we do it. Teaching democracy has to be more than just an afterthought. It needs to become something that we once again take seriously, celebrate informally as opportunities arise, and incorporate into our daily lives.

The beauty of it is that this can take on a lot of different forms. It should start with formal schooling. Studying the foundations of history and democracy in a classroom with a skilled educator is essential. Every year, in my Democratic Institutions seminar for law students, I have students who tell the story of how they fell in love with democracy in fourth- or sixth-grade civics classes. "I was hooked right there," a student told me a couple of years ago with a grin on her face. Teachers are among America's unsung heroes.

Beyond classroom basics, civics education can happen in our daily lives. If you belong to a book club, consider having a year of democracy studies, reading both fiction and nonfiction. Visit a museum with friends to see an exhibit that illuminates some facet of the American experience. Celebrate holidays like Independence Day, George Washington's Birthday, Juneteenth, Veterans Day, Labor Day, Memorial Day, and so on—really celebrate them in ways that put democracy center stage, so that we teach our children and remind ourselves about what really matters throughout the cycle of the year.

Imbue civics education with the meaning you want it to have, make it personal. You can teach your children about democracy when you take them along with you to vote. A trip to Washington, DC, or a virtual one, is an opportunity to experience the three branches of government. National holidays really can be more than days off work. My daughter, while in elementary school, took advantage of one Monday commemoration to sequester her two older brothers and me on the family trampoline, where she lectured us as she bounced up and down about the importance of her favorite holiday, Martin Luther King Jr. Day. She demanded that it be celebrated with the enthusiasm it merited. I've never been entirely certain where this came from. She spent a lot of Sunday mornings at church with her daddy, who belongs to a group called the United Fellowship Breakfast, which moves among some of the historic Black churches in Birmingham and provides some of the best fellowship I've ever experienced. It may be that she'd been listening carefully there or perhaps in school, but whatever it was, she felt the history and the spirit of community in her bones. It's never left her and because of her enthusiasm, I've always retained the feeling that it's an exceptionally important holiday. It must always be celebrated with a rereading of Dr. King's "Letter from Birmingham Jail," which she recited parts of to us on that day of celebration.

Democracy should be inherent in the memories we make—that's the best kind of civics education. Opportunities to teach and learn are all around us. Our goal is to instill a passion for democracy into our culture, so that we celebrate it as effortlessly and with as much intention as we do birthdays until it is no longer taken for granted. We can't allow that to happen again.

In the absence of a functional democracy girded by the rule of law, Americans would live at the whim of a king, which is just a nicer word for a dictator in this context. Elected representatives who foreswore their oaths and abandoned their constituents' best interests in service to those of the king would exist to woo the new royalty, and any benefit to their constituents would be entirely incidental. It's easy to understand why Madison and Hamilton were so determined to break free of the hold of both kings and factions. We need to continue to read their words today, and we need to live them.

Take some time and read for yourself about what the founders wanted for this country and why. Madison understood that some of those who became representatives of the people would fail. After he wrote in *Federalist* 51 that "if men were angels, no government would be necessary," he went further, acknowledging that because those same men who were not angels were involved in running government, there was reason for concern. "In framing a government which is to be administered by men over men, the great difficulty lies in this: you must first enable the government to control the governed; and the next place oblige it to control itself." In those few sentences, he captured the heart of the quandary. We should all take his words to heart.

We, the people, are the institution in the American republic where democracy can make a last stand when other institutions are frayed. We can check a runaway president with our protests and with our votes. If the Supreme Court absolves the president of the responsibilities everyone else has under the rule of law, holding him accountable at the ballot box is up to us. Supreme Court justices who find themselves in the minority on a case aren't the only ones who can dissent. We can too. But we can play that role in upholding our institutions only when we are properly informed about them.

RULES FOR THE CAVALRY

There are some guidelines for being in the cavalry—some modest rules that can help you keep your balance. Democracy is an ongoing experiment, which means that you have to prepare for it like it's a marathon. After the 2024 election, so many of us needed a respite, needed to unplug and recharge batteries. But the time for that is long gone. Now it's time to train.

Be Smart. Understand that forces that don't have your best interests at heart will try to manipulate you. They will do it with disinformation and use it on social media in a way that permits them to exploit fears and concerns. Our job is to resist being manipulated. Don't fall for the disinformation trap, where people with bad motives spread false information to inflame and provoke—to deceive. Disinformation is often spread further by people with no intent to do harm and who fall for the disinformation trap. The misinformation they spread also does damage. We've all seen it on Facebook or received it in an email from a well-meaning relative.

Finland developed a campaign to teach its schoolchildren media literacy so they could spot disinformation and misinformation. They are taught to read reports in the news and assess them before deciding whether to believe them, considering factors like the author's purpose, how and when the report was written, and what the author's central claims were. One Finnish teacher explained that she wanted her students to understand that "just because it's a good thing or it's a nice thing doesn't mean it's true or it's valid."

That deliberate emphasis on assessing the truthfulness and validity of information works. Of the forty-one European countries included in a survey on resilience in fighting misinformation, Finland was ranked at the top six years in a row. In 2023, the United States, Canada, Japan, Australia, South Korea, and Israel were added to the countries that were evaluated. The United States ranked seventeenth, while four Nordic countries, Estonia, and Ireland were at the top of the list. Canada was number seven.

Finland incorporates a focus on information accuracy into every subject that is taught until it becomes automatic. After successfully establishing the program for its students, the government expanded into adult education too. We don't have anything formal that approaches this in our country, but despite that—perhaps because of it—we can and should develop our own information literacy programs. Take up the study on your own or create a small group to work together. Make yourself as bulletproof as possible when it comes to disinformation, a tool that is used to destroy democracies. And demand that your school board adopt the Finnish model in our schools.

Be in Community. The old adage "Never worry alone" has new meaning. Being in community is part of how we survive the damage that is being inflicted on our country. Don't worry about democracy by yourself; share with friends. Especially if you're in a red state, or if you're frequently among people who don't share your concerns, surround yourself with people who take what we're facing seriously and who can buoy your spirits. Create a group that helps keep everyone informed, and find ways to take action together or serve your community. The grassroots are the real roots of our nation.

You don't have to fix the world alone. It's more fun, and you're more likely to succeed, if you get to work with other people who motivate you, teach you, and keep you going. It can be a virtual community like the one that's grown up online in the forum for my newsletter, "Civil Discourse," or it can be a real-world community that gets together in person. We all have different situations. The important thing is finding the people who will sustain you and let you sustain them too.

Never Bet against America. Refuse to believe that government doesn't work. We elect representatives to do a job. It's time to stop tolerating poor performance and acting as though there's nothing we can do about it. It's time to make demands of the people who are supposed to be representing us, whether or not we're from the same party. Don't let your members of Congress off easy. Their job is to represent all their constituents, not just the ones who voted for them, and your job is to make sure they understand that. Send them an annotated copy of *The Federalist Papers* if they're acting like they need a refresher.

This also goes for state and local officials. Don't make it easy for them to do their jobs poorly. Demand. Be heard. Call and write daily if you have the energy. Show up in groups; take all your friends along. It's time to insist on good government.

Understand That Protecting Democracy Comes in a Lot of Flavors. Democracy is about the ability of individuals to act on their own views and beliefs. Different issues matter to different people. If everyone devotes their energy to the issues that matter most to them, then all the work gets done. And it doesn't have to be strictly political. Some people will support democracy through the arts. They will write songs and plays; they will paint and knit. If we do this right, we encourage people to find their best approach while we commit to ours.

Go out and protest if that works for you, but remember you can voice your support for democracy in other ways too. We've talked about registering voters, but you can also volunteer as a tutor for kids in under-resourced schools or as a language teacher for new immigrants. Donate your time or money to a local food bank, help veterans, volunteer with programs for the elderly, be a clinic escort. Whether you're making big purchases or buying weekly groceries, shop at places that align with your values.

Decide Who You Are and Stick to It. Danielle Sassoon knew. So did Hagan Scotten. Sassoon was the acting U.S. Attorney for the Southern District of New York at the start of the second Trump administration. She resigned when she was told to dismiss a public corruption case the office had brought against New York's mayor, a case that, in her judgment, was solid. She was concerned it was being dismissed because of the White House's political agenda, something that should never interfere with justice. Scotten was an assistant U.S. Attorney who worked for Sassoon. He resigned too. They both knew where their personal lines in the sand were. They didn't compromise their integrity, even when it meant walking away from jobs they loved.

Sassoon and Scotten both understood that they couldn't follow orders they knew were wrong and come out intact. It's a lesson the Republican Party as a whole failed to grasp when it succumbed to Trump in 2016. After the first compromise, you face the same death by a thousand cuts over and over again.

We all need to decide who we are. Know your personal red lines. Be prepared to make a stand for them. Once you cave in, like some law firms and universities did when Trump came to them with demands, that's who you are.

Be the Hope. We know progress isn't always linear. Some days are bad days. If things look hopeless, be the hope. Help others get over the rough patches. We all go through them. Things may look bad, but if you give up, there is no chance of succeeding in the end. The only option is to keep going.

Take Baby Steps. It might not seem like enough, but it can be the slow, individual, person-to-person conversations that matter the most. Plant seeds that might grow down the road. They might sit there for a long time, even years, until events touch a person and make those seeds start to grow. Then, when the person you've been patiently talking to knows someone who gets deported, or the person loses their job, or there is an absent Social Security check, the seeds get their chance. Trust that once planted, your seeds will grow.

Believe that the work you are doing is important, because it is. The steps we take as individuals add up. They're an effective form of collective action that it's easy to underestimate. We are not fighting Nazis on a battlefield in Europe; we are fighting in the voting booths in our own country, trying to win the hearts and minds of fellow citizens.

A couple of years ago, after another week of hectic travel, I was flying out of Reagan Airport in Washington, DC, headed home. It was crowded and everyone seemed eager to leave. You could feel the concern about the Biden campaign and the possibility that Trump might return to office circulating in the terminal. Just when I wasn't expecting it, I encountered a powerful form of pro-democracy advocacy. The woman in line in front of me was engaging in a little quiet civil discourse. She'd decorated her backpack with buttons emblazoned with slogans that included:

"Democracy is not a spectator sport"

"Protect the vote"

"Women's liberation" (this one on a pink background with a red Statue of Liberty putting a sturdy fist forward to show both her power and her interest in connecting with other women)

It was an eloquent reminder. I saw it register around me on other people's faces. If you believe in democracy, you're not alone. Your seeds could be a bumper sticker, a T-shirt, or a printed bookmark you leave for someone to pick up. Your words of reassurance, baby steps, will make a difference.

Exercise Your Rights. Protest works. It is quintessentially American. We have a First Amendment right to peacefully assemble and petition the government, to speak freely, to associate with whom we choose.

I'm sure you heard some of the same whispers I heard. "Maybe we shouldn't go out and protest; he might impose the Insurrection Act." "Protest doesn't work anymore; times have changed." It's just like voting; no one works so hard to take away your rights—or better yet, to get you to give them up on your own—unless they make a difference, and this one does. Exercise it early and often. And take your friends along with you.

WHAT IS THE CAVALRY CAPABLE OF?

In early 2025, the Trump administration canceled a Marine Band concert. The Marine Band, called "The President's Own," had held a contest the previous year in which they selected thirty students to play at a concert with them. But there was one problem. The new administration decided that the concert ran afoul of executive orders that prohibited the government from continuing what it designated as DEI programs, short for "diversity, equity, and inclusion." The new administration prohibited anything that smacked of diversity, and the young musicians selected were Black, Hispanic, Indian, and Asian.

What happened next was classic. The CBS news show *60 Minutes* decided to fly the young musicians to Washington, DC, to interview them. The people who had connected the young musicians with the Marine Band in the first place reached out to military band retirees. When the retirees learned what had happened, a group of them flew in from across the country to play a concert with the students in the nation's capital. Former band members from the Army, Navy, Air Force, Coast Guard, West Point, the Naval Academy, and the Marines all joined in. *60 Minutes* decided to air the concert. A performance that might have been seen by only a few hundred people in person ended up garnering millions of viewers on national television. It was a lot of fun. It was civics in action.

The curious thing about living through a full-blown constitutional crisis is that for those who want to, or are just distracted by pressing obligations, it's remarkably easy to ignore. An acquaintance texted early on, "If I don't watch, maybe it's not actually happening." Early 2025 was a frustrating time for people who were focused on what was going on and knew it was not normal. Still, restaurants were full, people walked their dogs, watched their children graduate, went to work, took European vacations, and watched as college basketball season gave way to baseball. Things looked reasonably normal, or at least they did if you didn't look too hard at the rough edges, like the masked ICE agents coming after people on American streets.

It can feel like you're weightless in the middle of a constitutional crisis if you aren't yet directly affected; it's easy to float away and leave it behind. There wasn't a dictator sitting on a throne in the public square, dramatically crossing out broad swaths of the Constitution with his Sharpie marker. There wasn't a dramatic crisis like the one we watched in South Korea, where members of the National Assembly scrambled past barriers to return to work and vote down a coup. In the United States, developments were cloaked in a thin veneer of legality, and for many people it was easier to hope it would stop, or hope that the courts would stop it before it went too far, than to confront the reality of the moment.

What do you do when there is no national awakening on

the horizon? You can hope for an acute crisis that forces a reckoning—and there were those who thought it might come in the form of Trump supporters experiencing higher prices or damaged supply chains. Perhaps that crisis still will come or maybe it already has by the time you are reading these words. But fixing democracy is not something that happens neatly in an hourlong time slot like an episode of *Law & Order*. It takes many conversations, sometimes easy but more often difficult, between Americans—people who know and trust one another, and who develop an awareness that spreads across the country. It requires persistence.

As President Reagan said:

> Freedom is never more than one generation away from extinction. We didn't pass it on to our children in the bloodstream. The only way they can inherit the freedom we have known is if we fight for it, protect it, defend it, and then hand it to them with the well-taught lessons of how they in their lifetime must do the same. And if you and I don't do this, then you and I may well spend our sunset years telling our children and our children's children what it was once like in America where men were free.

President Biden put it more succinctly: "Democracy is never guaranteed. Every generation must preserve it, defend it, and fight for it."

Each of us has the obligation to figure out what we're going to do, where it makes sense for us to slot in, given our personal circumstances. I don't have a monopoly on answers. But I understand that the hardest part can be getting started. That's what I hope this book will encourage you to do. You don't need a big platform or a lot of resources. You don't have to solve the entire problem on your own. Because when we are a community, together, we can be one hell of a cavalry.

What we can't afford to do is give up and walk away. We can't pretend it will get better without intentional action on our part. We cannot leave the heavy lifting to others. All of us who believe in democracy must find ways to work together and to do whatever we can, whenever opportunity places itself in front of us, to hold on to the Republic. Lawyers are not the entire answer to this problem; democracy belongs to all of us. But lawyers do have a special responsibility to their communities. We can draw some inspiration there.

LAW DAY

Every year on May 1, Law Day is observed nationwide. It's a celebration of the rule of law, a day for lawyers to reach out and provide civics education in their communities. Law Day was the brainchild of American Bar Association President Charles S. Rhyne and was established by President Dwight D. Eisenhower in 1958. Eisenhower wrote in his proclamation, "I urge the people of the United States to observe the designated day with appropriate ceremonies and activities; and I especially urge the legal profession, the press and the radio, television and motion picture industries to promote and to participate in the observance of that day."

That's what has happened ever since. The American Bar Association holds high-level gatherings. State bars across the country hold events. Thousands of lawyers speak to students about the importance of the rule of law. Some courts and community groups join in. It's a day devoted to spreading understanding about what it means to have a government under law. Lawyers tell students stories about their cases and their work in and out of court.

It's not enough, just that one day. But it's the right idea. What we really need is to have Law Day every day. We need a culture where the rule of law is understood and respected, so it can flourish again. The primary reason "it's about the economy, stupid" rang true is that up until now, we've been able to take the continued existence of democracy for granted. Right now it's democracy, but we need to be smart about it.

Lawyers can start this work, although ultimately, we must all take responsibility for it. Lawyers take an oath when they are admitted to the bar, and although the precise language varies from jurisdiction to jurisdiction, it includes a promise to uphold the Constitution and our laws. What better way to do that than by recommitting to civics education in troubled times?

LET ME TELL YOU ABOUT A CONVERSATION I HAD WITH MY YOUN-gest child, who was born in 2002. He was a college senior at the time. What would it take, I wondered, to get people like him—smart, well educated, possibly more interested in football and video games than politics, but decent, caring people—to want to read a book about saving democracy? He listened to my question, smiled patiently, and explained that as long as he had been alive, there hadn't *been* a real democracy, that people with power and influence controlled everything.

Why shouldn't he try to make it better? I asked him.

"I know I'm a know-nothing twenty-two-year-old," he said. "What can I do against the power of Congress and caucuses? It makes me angry. It feels like an insult when you tell us to stand up and do something. The opposition is millionaire congressmen with connections, even on the state level."

That pulled me up short. For the first time, I understood that his generation lacked the attachment to democracy mine has. Even people who weren't fully included in democracy could understand its promise when I was his age, and they wanted it for themselves. But many younger people don't feel the deep moral imperative to save democracy like we do, because their experience of it has been different. It's not all young people, but it is enough of them. When I asked him about making it better, he told me, "Protests don't work. That's something your generation thinks. I was four when Occupy Wall Street happened. Nothing has changed since." How is he supposed to value democracy when his first decade of political awareness has largely consisted of watching a growing consolidation of wealth and power among the few, seeing the rise of a president who doesn't believe in democracy, and being tolerated by courts and a Congress that won't fight for it?

I'm not certain his views have changed yet, but I know he's watching the protests that have sprung up across the country with interest and perhaps even a little newfound hope. He told me recently that he *hoped* the protests would work. His generation needs more than history lessons. We have to be candid with them about the flaws that have emerged in our democracy if we're going to rebuild stronger. We have to set high expectations for how a functioning democracy should operate—expectations that don't leave room for kleptocracy or kakistocracy. The Founding Fathers set high standards. We should insist upon them.

Younger generations believe democracy has failed them, and they don't believe it can be fixed because they've never seen it happen. Dictators are propaganda lords. They are singularly talented at persuading people who have become complacent about the value of democracy in their lives that there are no consequences to losing it. They are masters of making promises they can't keep and walking away from them without consequence when the truth comes to light. They are skilled at exploiting economic and social unrest and political dissatisfaction.

Ultimately, the only way a dictator can hold power is by controlling the flow of information and resorting to the spread of disinformation that serves his purposes and permits him to retain authority. Education about country and the Constitution—simple, easy to do over an afternoon snack or a family dinner as well as in the classroom—is an important part of fighting back. Education is an antidote to the creeping sickness that lets too many in our country turn a blind eye to inconsistency and hypocrisy and, in doing so, makes autocracy possible, even plausible. We owe it to our kids to resist. We owe it to them to get it right.

Professor E. Doyle Stevick studies democratic backsliding in formerly communist Eastern European countries, such as Hungary and Poland, which adopted democracy after the dissolution of the Soviet bloc. Hungary, as we've discussed, is now an "illiberal democracy." Poland, in June 2025, saw elections that resulted in victory for a president characterized as pro-Trump. Stevick's view is that if new democracies fail to fully understand and embrace the rule of law, they're at risk of being "vulnerable and incomplete." They need a cultural transformation in order for the change to take hold.

Our situation in the United States, with a well-established tradition of democracy, is somewhat different. We require a reinvigoration of the culture we have but have set aside. But the basics remain the same as for Eastern Europe: The public must embrace the rule of law for democracy to succeed, and education is the most promising way to ensure that it happens and that it sticks for future generations.

Stevick writes that "the most promising avenues for advancing rule of law norms come not from additional reform to traditional instruction, i.e., civic education courses, but from direct experiences of civic participation, including within the classroom and school." It comes down to creating a culture where knowledge about democracy and how our form of government functions is the norm. Hands-on experience with democracy is essential. That's our road map for getting civics education right. We need to be a country of lifetime civics learners.

The founder of Law Day, Charles Rhyne, saw the timeless value of the rule of law. He viewed it in the context of the Cold War, seeing the contrast between democracy and communism. The words he chose in his original Law Day speech in 1958 have ironic resonance today:

> This liberty and equality through our systems of government under law stands in stark contrast to the system of government by Communism where the tyranny and caprice of Communist leaders hold all men in constant terror. In America law reigns supreme. No man in our Country is above law, not even the President of the United States. In Russia the Kremlin rulers are not only above the law but they are "the law" just as were the Czars and Kings of ancient times. The rulers under Communism govern by might alone. Government by terror does not exist in America and cannot exist under our government of law.

Decades later, in a speech he gave on Law Day in May 2000, Rhyne, who was by then in his late eighties, told the story of how Law Day came to pass. According to Rhyne, President Eisenhower's chief of staff, Sherman Adams, was morally opposed to having his boss sign anything "praising lawyers." Rhyne explained he got around that by walking out of Adams's office and straight down the hall into the Oval Office (it was a different era!) for a second opinion.

> The President held his hand up for silence until he had read the entire document. Then he said, "Sherm, this Proclamation does not contain one word praising lawyers. It praises our constitutional system of government, our great heritage under the rule of law, and asks our people to stand up and praise what they have created. I like it and I am going to sign it." And he did.

Rhyne closed his speech by issuing a challenge. He said he hoped that Law Day could provide an opportunity to "explore ways in which not only the Internet, but also other new technologies, can make more law more readily available to those who need it." So much of what we see about the transmission of information on the internet involves concerns about misinformation and disinformation. But it doesn't have to be that way. We should take up Rhyne's challenge and use technology to make accurate information about the rule of law and democracy accessible. Bar associations can expand the concept of Law Day and become full-time advocates for democracy who use their profession as an opportunity to take on responsibility for educating the public. Democracy isn't a waterwheel that will continue to turn on its own without our involvement. It requires care and fine-tuning. And most of all, it requires people who know it and people who love it.

One of the most powerful slogans Democrats used in the 2024 election was "We are not going back." We should keep using it. We should refuse to accept efforts to roll back gains we've made as a country. Executive orders can impact the executive branch of government, but they can't tell citizens what to think or feel or how to behave. They have no force over us. Canceling celebrations of Black History Month? Canceling the work of women who served in the military and moved this country forward? Those are acts of cowardice. The Defense Department may have halted its observation of Holocaust Days of Remembrance, Juneteenth, Black History Month, Pride Month, and Martin Luther King Jr. Day, among others, because of Donald Trump's executive orders, but we don't need his permission to celebrate our fellow citizens' contributions to our country. As Americans, we have that right and we should exercise it, joyfully and together.

Cultivate an ability to resist senseless attacks like this on our culture. Fascism's Achilles' heel is the power of citizens who are ready to use it. Don't give up hope. Pick one small thing you can do this week and get started. And then keep going.

Conclusion

It was a beautiful morning in March 2025, one of those days when the sun comes out following a storm and the plants are all a luminous green. It was the kind of day that makes you want to linger outside. But I had a lot to do, and I forced myself to go into the office. I was rewarded with an amazing email in my inbox from a reader of my newsletter. She wrote about seeing Norman Rockwell's classic 1943 paintings *Four Freedoms* with her grandson a few weeks earlier. The "freedoms" in the paintings are *Freedom of Speech*, *Freedom from Fear*, *Freedom from Want*, and *Freedom of Worship*. Even though my reader was very familiar with the paintings, seeing them with her grandson was like seeing them again for the first time. What hit her was the realization that she had always taken those freedoms for granted. Like many of us, she didn't fully realize that until the moment when they were under attack.

We are seeing now how essential it is that we keep our eyes and our actions focused on preserving these freedoms. We have to make sure we don't backslide, like the frogs. I'm increasingly confident that we can get there, that we are now living in a country where democracy has taken center stage as a campaign issue. The traditional advice given by political pollsters that Americans don't care about democracy is belied by the No Kings marches and the Tesla protests. The people who stood against Elon Musk, who protested the random destruction of government agencies like USAID and the Department of Education, who marched for science and medicine—we put our love of America and the Constitution on full display. Americans understand democracy, and now more of us understand what losing it would mean. Deep in our bones, we feel the urge to protect it and keep it. To the extent that traditional wisdom says Americans won't vote for democracy, it's wrong. We are fighting for it every day.

Now it's time to do the hard work—stay informed, stay engaged, and bring others along with us. We need to be fearless about talking with the people around us and explaining why our democracy matters, the damage that is being done to it, and what we can do to protect it. I don't expect our progress to be immediate. Nothing worth having ever is! We are in it for keeps, not just for the next term of the Supreme Court or the next election. We must persevere.

In the end, it comes down to a simple kernel of truth: We cannot give up.

So, where does the strength to keep going come from when we've already lived through an insurrection and no one has been held accountable? When we live in a time in which we teeter on the edge of multiple constitutional crises constantly stoked by the president himself?

We keep the Republic by being stubborn and steadfast. We don't need clickbait-style, attention-grabbing headlines to make the pursuit of civics and democracy be deeply satisfying. We can decide that we will deliberately spend some of our time tuned in to our history and the study of our laws, because that framework can make a real difference in how we understand the news that comes at us fast, every day. Instead of falling into hopelessness and anxiety, we can chart a course through this moment and out the other side.

That other side is coming, even though it's hard to believe it some days. When it gets here, the challenge will be making sure we do everything we can to restore and protect democracy from future attack. It's exciting, this prospect of revitalizing our democracy. It will be the kind of work that restores the soul. It can be our generation's legacy.

PRESIDENTS DON'T HOLD ONE-ON-ONE PRIVATE MEETINGS ABOUT cases with U.S. attorneys, or at least they didn't during my tenure at the Justice Department, during the Obama administration and earlier. We saw the president rarely and in formal, public settings for the most part. That's how I found myself in the East Wing of the White House, lining up with my colleagues from across the country, to hear what the president, our boss, had to say to us. When Barack Obama strode into the room with his White House counsel, a former prosecutor herself, at his side, all the confidence and easy charisma he brought to the presidency were on display. He had a shout-out for the U.S. Attorney in Chicago, his hometown. But then he turned serious. He looked at all of us carefully to make sure we understood that what he was about to say was important. "I appointed you," he said, "but you don't serve me. You serve the American people. And I expect you to act with independence and integrity."

That was exactly what I wanted to do. When you're a United States attorney, your job involves prosecuting crimes and defending the United States when it gets sued. But when it comes down to it, the job is to protect people's civil rights. That means making sure that a criminal defendant accused of the most horrific crimes still receives due process. That means guaranteeing that victims' rights are protected. That means challenging state laws that would strip people of their rights, like the voting rights cases I worked on or DOJ's challenge to Alabama's deeply flawed "deport yourself" anti-immigrant bill in 2011.

It's an extraordinary thing to have that opportunity to serve, to uphold country and Constitution. And when you work for DOJ, the opportunity to do that is yours every day. That's the job.

Our current situation is difficult. But even though no one has hired us to do it, we all have an equally important role to play, the job of keeping the Republic. The opportunities may be less obvious—no one will assign us a case to prosecute. It's up to us to seek out those opportunities and get to work. In the Justice Department we say: Do the right thing, for the right reasons, in the right way. That's the essence of how all of us should move forward now, in this moment when our country needs us.

If you love America, and I do, you never really leave government service. It was the honor of my lifetime to serve in the Justice Department and in the Obama administration. I wrote this book as part of my ongoing commitment, part call to arms, part how-to manual. Now it's your turn. Let's go fight for the country we love, not on a battlefield but with understanding, ideas, and commitment. It's our time to serve.

Postscript

On June 27, 2025, the Supreme Court ended its term with a bang. One of its final decisions, *Trump v. CASA*, stalled the use of nationwide injunctions, a key tool lawyers had wielded to push back against the Trump administration's unconstitutional excesses. Although lawyers litigating against the administration proved nimble, coming up with new strategies like class-action certifications, the public's already flagging confidence in the Supreme Court was damaged further by the 6–3 decision. Judges, lawyers, and legal scholars on both sides of the political divide had expressed concerns about nationwide injunctions over the years, but the Court decided against their use only when it benefited the Trump administration. Back in 2024, the Biden administration had asked the Court to address the issue of nationwide injunctions blocking their efforts at student loan relief, but the Court declined to take that case. It is fair to ask why the Court decided to intervene now.

This outcome suggested an ominous possibility to many observers—that no matter what the issue was, the Supreme Court would always weigh in for Trump, and worse, that the other two branches of government, Congress and the courts, were fully aligned with, if not outright captives of the executive.

Nominally, the issue in *Trump v. CASA* was whether it was constitutional for Donald Trump to end birthright citizenship, which is guaranteed by the Fourteenth Amendment to the Constitution. But the solicitor general's office successfully maneuvered the Court into hearing only the issue of whether a judge could enter a nationwide injunction to stop any action taken by a president, divorcing that question, at least for the time being, from the underlying action taken by Trump, which virtually all legal scholars agreed exceeded his authority. Presidents can't amend the Constitution. There is a well-established, lengthy process for doing that, one that requires both Congress and state legislatures.

Justice Sotomayor's dissenting response was unrelenting: "The rule of law is not a given in this Nation, nor any other," she wrote. "It is a precept of our democracy that will endure only if those brave enough in every branch fight for its survival. Today, the Court abdicates its vital role in that effort. With the stroke of a pen, the President has made a 'solemn mockery' of our Constitution. . . . Rather than stand firm, the Court gives way. Because such complicity should know no place in our system of law, I dissent."

Her words went to the heart of the moment.

Just days earlier, on June 12, Washington Senator Patty Murray rose on the floor of the Senate to condemn the treatment of fellow Democratic Senator Alex Padilla of California, who was manhandled out of a press conference held by Department of Homeland Security Secretary Kristi Noem, taken to the ground and handcuffed, after attempting to ask her a question. Murray was unequivocal in her remarks: "This is what a democracy is about . . . it is about us coming to the United States Senate, speaking out, asking questions, getting information, so we can be their [the people's] voice. What happens when that voice is stifled? What happens when that voice is thrown to the floor and handcuffed? . . . We are a democracy, but we can lose that democracy. It can be gone, unless all of us speak out and forcibly reject what happened to a United States Senator."

Murray decried the failure of Republican senators to join their Democratic colleagues in condemning Padilla's treatment, while Republicans largely sought to dodge by victim-blaming Padilla. Much like Justice Sotomayor, Murray was left expressing sorrow and outrage that her branch of government was abandoning its constitutional obligations in the face of the Trump administration's misconduct.

But no matter how hard the Trump administration seemed to be trying, neither of these brave Americans was giving up, and neither can we. Consider California Judge Charles Breyer. On the same day that Senator Murray was speaking out against her colleague's violent treatment, Judge Breyer was pushing back against the Trump administration's assertion of unfettered authority to send in federalized troops to Los

Angeles to put down protests against Immigration and Customs Enforcement (ICE). California Governor Gavin Newsom, who had strenuously objected to the deployment, sued. When the Trump administration argued that the president's decision was final and not subject to review by any entity, even the courts, Breyer's reaction during an emergency hearing was: "That's not where we live. We live in response to a monarch. This country was founded in response to a monarch." Presidents, quite explicitly in our system, are not kings and are not meant to become kings. Trump's attempts to act like a king are illegal. If we believe in the Constitution, we will not abide them.

Whether Breyer's decision in the case ultimately stands up in the Supreme Court remains to be seen, but his sentiment is enduring, a reminder that Americans explicitly rejected being subject to a monarchy when they adopted our form of government and embraced the Constitution. No president may assume monarchical powers. Legal scholars have cautioned across the years that the Constitution is not a suicide pact. Article II cannot be said to establish the president as a monarch or a dictator, because the origin story of our nation reclaims power for the people and not a privileged few.

As I was finishing up this book, things seemed to keep getting worse. Who could have imagined an American president touting a detention camp built in a Florida swamp, surrounded by alligators, to house migrants being processed for deportation? "It's known as Alligator Alcatraz, which is very appropriate because I looked outside and that's not a place I want to go hiking," Trump said. Who could have imagined our democratic government deporting people to dangerous countries that aren't their place of origin? This administration has chosen to drop deported human beings into South Sudan, a country on the brink of civil war, which the US State Department warns Americans not to travel to because of the risk of kidnapping and murder. Our government shouldn't be able to consign people to conditions in a foreign country that it actively seeks to protect its own citizens from. This is unconscionable behavior. And this is just the start.

Those of us who understand what we are seeing have a solemn obligation to speak out and share that truth with others. Change is possible. Much like how people who served in the first Trump administration grew disenchanted, left, and even took up the torch against him—people like Mike Pence's advisor Olivia Troye, and former Joint Chiefs chairman General Mark Milley—so many of our fellow citizens have begun to see the light as Trump's abuses hit closer to home, even if they're not all yet willing to say so out loud. Remind Trump's reluctant supporters that no one foresaw Americans losing government jobs and desperately needed medical care when they voted for Trump, and it's their right to change their minds and part ways with him. It may take a concrete experience like seeing a favorite local waitress or a child's fourth grade classmate deported, or the loss of a government job because of who their friends are, for people to open themselves up to the reality of what is happening in America.

Never give up on talking with the people around you, the ones who have decided to look away and tolerate what's happening. Today it's immigrants and transgender people; tomorrow it could just as easily be them. An autocrat like Trump would turn the power of the presidency into a tool for keeping people in line, for preventing dissent—from anyone. Today he attacks groups he thinks many people won't have sympathy for or those that can't successfully fight back, but it doesn't stop there. Ultimately, the target is anyone who won't give way. It's all of us.

Many people will still pass these warnings off as fearmongering. But tell that to the students whose visas have been canceled, to the ones who no longer feel safe trying to travel, and to the prospective students who no longer want to risk applying to come here in the first place. Tell that to transgender children who are being denied gender-affirming care. Tell that to the people in a Salvadoran prison whose stories we don't know because they are being held incommunicado. What happens to anyone who gets in a dictator's way?

This moment challenges us to understand how our system of government works, what rights it gives us, and how we can use our power to ensure that tyranny cannot take permanent hold in this country. I hope this book can play a small role in helping us hold the line and defend democracy. At the end of the day, it takes more than people in powerful positions to hold a president who wants to become a strongman in check. It will take all of us. It will be the small acts of protest, of resistance, of education, and of love for country that will keep the dictator from seizing control. It may not always be your turn to save democracy, but it's always your turn to be present, to do whatever you can, and to support the people who do the work to keep the Republic. The dictator's most dangerous weapon is his ability to overwhelm us with the feeling that we are helpless by keeping up an endless on-slaught of terrible things. We can neutralize that weapon by knowing our own strength and saying no to feeling power-less. What we must do, then, is obvious. We must persist until we succeed. Make your love of this country, despite her im-perfections, relentless and refuse to give that up. American citizenship confers a great responsibility. We must do our best, together, to live up to it.

Acknowledgments

I could not have written this book without support from a large community of caring people, and I am deeply grateful.

To Alli, for her amazing research.

To Katie, for her skillful editing.

To the Durkans—everyone should have a group of friends this wonderful. And also to Mary, Katie, Eugene, Jen, and Kathy, who believed in me and gave me really great advice and hugs when I needed them.

To Elie, who shared important details about book-writing with me.

To my podcast sisters, Barb, Kim, and Jill, and our amazing team. They lifted me up constantly.

To Preet, Tamara, and the rest of our team. By keeping me intellectually rigorous on issues that could have easily slid into emotion, you all make me so much better every day.

Acknowledgments

To my amazing agent, Jen Rohrer, who is a friend, not just my agent; and to my wonderful book agent, Christy Fletcher, who made this dream real. None of this would have happened without Nick Amphlett, who believed in this book and understood that it needed to happen before I did. To Jane, who helped me at the end, when I needed it the most. And to the cavalry at Dutton, who designed and produced this book and then helped me share it with the world.

To Laura, the most cheerful human being I know, and to Sarah, who baked for me even though she was working on her own book. So many people in our neighborhood helped at different points along the way.

To my wonderful colleagues at MSNBC. I could not be prouder to be a part of such a distinguished group or more nourished by the ideas and arguments I was exposed to.

To my Jewish sisters, my moral center.

To my knitting friends, who stuck with me despite my sporadic knitting and off-topic conversations while I was working on the book.

To the numerous locals in Birmingham who saw me writing in a coffee shop and cheered me on.

To Venessa and Jim, who are always smart and especially staunch.

To Catherine, who is a constant source of common sense, good writing advice, and affection.

To my childhood best friend Sara, who offered unconditional support.

And to my husband, Bob, and our kids, who unerringly believed in me (most of the time) and told me their best stories, argued with me about the right thing to do, and kept me in line with their practical, no-nonsense love. My family doesn't believe in settling for easy answers and they didn't let me do that here. Also, thanks, Bob, for that one time you brought me a latte.

Notes

CHAPTER 1: DON'T BE THE FROG

10   **more than 140 executive orders:** Fin Daniel Gómez and Anne Bryson, "Trump Sets Executive Order Record in His First 100 Days," CBS News, April 29, 2025, https://www.cbsnews.com/news/trump-first-100-days-executive-order-record/.

11   **he said as much:** Lauren Camera, "Trump's Latest Campaign Pledge: Revenge," *U.S. News & World Report*, June 7, 2024, https://www.usnews.com/news/national-news/articles/2024-06-07/trumps-latest-campaign-pledge-revenge.

12   **"find" him enough votes:** Michael D. Shear and Stephanie Saul, "Trump, in Taped Call, Pressured Georgia Official to 'Find' Votes to Overturn Election," *New York Times*, January 3, 2021, https://www.nytimes.com/2021/01/03/us/politics/trump-raffensperger-call-georgia.html.

12   **than a George Wallace:** Stephen Smith and Kate Ellis, "George C. Wallace: Powerful Third-Party Candidate," *American Public*

Media Reports, accessed June 25, 2025, https://features.apmre ports.org/arw/campaign68/d1.html.

12 **or a Lyndon LaRouche:** James Doubek, "Conspiracy Theorist and Frequent Presidential Candidate Lyndon LaRouche Dies at 96," NPR, February 14, 2019, https://www.npr.org/2019/02 /14/694626800/conspiracy-theorist-and-frequent-presiden tial-candidate-lyndon-larouche-dies-at/.

12 *The Washington Post:* Isaac Arnsdorf, Josh Dawsey, and Devlin Barrett, "Trump and Allies Plot Revenge, Justice Department Control in a Second Term," *Washington Post*, November 5, 2023, https://www.washingtonpost.com/politics/2023/11/05/trump -revenge-second-term/.

12 **right-wing think tank:** Steve Contorno, "Trump Claims Not to Know Who Is Behind Project 2025," CNN, July 11, 2024, https://www.cnn.com/2024/07/11/politics/trump-allies -project-2025/index.html.

14 **James Madison titled *Federalist* 51:** James Madison, *Federalist*, no. 51, in *The Federalist Papers*, ed. Clinton Rossiter (New American Library, 1961), 320.

14 **echoes of Montesquieu's belief:** Montesquieu, "Book XI: Of the Laws Which Establish Political Liberty, with Regard to the Constitution," in *The Spirit of the Laws*, trans. Thomas Nugent (1758).

14 **Madison's famous line:** Madison, *Federalist*, no. 61, 322.

15 **He wrote in *Federalist* 47:** Madison, *Federalist*, no. 47, 301.

15 **The lawsuits, which involved:** "Trump Administration Liti gation Tracker," *Lawfare*, accessed June 25, 2025, https://www .lawfaremedia.org/projects-series/trials-of-the-trump -administration/tracking-trump-administration-litigation.

16 **do is "kill all the lawyers":** Olivia Rutigliano, "What Did Shakespeare Mean When He Wrote 'Let's Kill All the Lawyers'?,"

Literary Hub, January 25, 2023, https://lithub.com/what-did
-shakespeare-mean-when-he-wrote-lets-kill-all-the-lawyers/.

17   **free legal advice:** "President Donald J. Trump Directs Suspen-
sion of Security Clearances and Evaluation of Government
Contracts for Involvement in Government Weaponization,"
fact sheet, The White House, February 25, 2025, https://www
.whitehouse.gov/fact-sheets/2025/02/fact-sheet-president
-donald-j-trump-directs-suspension-of-security-clearances
-and-evaluation-of-government-contracts-for-involvement
-in-government-weaponization/.

17   **came for more firms:** John R. Vile, "Trump's Executive Orders against Law Firms," Free Speech Center, March 28, 2025,
https://firstamendment.mtsu.edu/article/trumps-executive
-orders-against-law-firms/.

17   **unlawful "racial discrimination":** "Addressing Risks from
WilmerHale," executive order, The White House, March 27,
2025, https://www.whitehouse.gov/presidential-actions/2025
/03/addressing-risks-from-wilmerhale/.

18   **under the restrictive provisions:** "Addressing Risks from
Paul Weiss," The White House, March 14, 2025, https://www
.whitehouse.gov/presidential-actions/2025/03/addressing
-risks-from-paul-weiss/.

18   **from publicly naming them:** Melissa Quinn, "Trump's Cru-
sade against Big Law Firms Sparks Fears of Long-Lasting
Damage," CBS News, April 2, 2025, https://www.cbsnews.com
/news/trumps-big-law-firms-retribution/.

18   **"many firms take actions":** "Addressing Risks from Wilmer-
Hale."

18   **"yet another law firm":** "Addressing Risks from WilmerHale."

19   **even a whistleblower complaint:** "Protected Whistleblower
Disclosure of Erez Reuveni Regarding Violation of Laws,

Rules & Regulations, Abuse of Authority, and Substantial and Specific Danger to Health and Safety at the Department of Justice," Government Accountability Project, June 24, 2025, https://statico1.nyt.com/newsgraphics/documenttools/e285ec96adf8d443/5868d536-full.pdf.

20   **they should be impeached:** Lawrence Hurley, "Chief Justice Pushes Back against Calls to Impeach Judges Who Rule against Trump," NBC News, March 18, 2025, https://www.nbcnews.com/politics/supreme-court/chief-justice-pushes-back-calls-impeach-judges-rule-trump-rcna196922.

20   **Justice Samuel Alito relied on:** Ken Armstrong, "Draft Overturning Roe v. Wade Quotes Infamous Witch Trial Judge with Long-Discredited Ideas on Rape," *ProPublica*, May 6, 2022, https://www.propublica.org/article/abortion-roe-wade-alito-scotus-hale.

21   **George Washington stepped down:** John Ferling, *Adams v. Jefferson: The Tumultuous Election of 1800* (Oxford University Press, 2004), 85.

21   **Accusations flew that the winner:** Peter Reichard, "The Rise of 'Faction': The Presidential Election of 1800 Set the Standard for Acrimony," Sutherland Institute, July 18, 2024, https://sutherlandinstitute.org/the-rise-of-faction-the-presidential-election-of-1800-set-the-standard-for-acrimony/.

21   **Judiciary Act of 1801:** "*Marbury v. Madison*: The Empowerment of the Judiciary," Supreme Court Historical Society, accessed May 14, 2025, https://supremecourthistory.org/schs-marbury-madison-empowerment-of-the-judiciary/.

22   **seventeen new justices of the peace:** "*Marbury v. Madison*."

22   **"an outrage on decency":** "*Marbury v. Madison*."

22   **Adams had provided:** "*Marbury v. Madison*."

22   **"whose views are to defeat mine":** "*Marbury v. Madison*."

23   **in the Judiciary Act of 1789:** "Federal Judiciary Act (1789),"

National Archives, May 10, 2022, https://www.archives.gov /milestone-documents/federal-judiciary-act.

23   **the Court's unanimous opinion:** Marbury v. Madison, 5 U.S. 137 (1803).

24   **"supreme law of the land":** *Marbury*, 5 U.S. at 180.

24   **the Constitution that controls:** *Marbury*, 5 U.S. at 177.

25   *Youngstown Sheet & Tube Co. v. Sawyer*: Youngstown Sheet & Tube Co. v. Sawyer, 343 U.S. 579 (1952).

25   **at war in Korea:** "A Short History of the Korean War," Imperial War Museums, accessed May 14, 2025, https://www.iwm .org.uk/history/a-short-history-of-the-korean-war.

25   **the United Steelworkers of America:** *Youngstown*, 343 U.S. at 582–83.

25   **a nationwide strike:** *Youngstown*, 343 U.S. at 583.

25   **"The indispensability of steel":** *Youngstown*, 343 U.S. at 583.

26   **fight off the executive order:** *Youngstown*, 343 U.S. at 583.

26   **especially Article II of the Constitution:** *Youngstown*, 343 U.S. at 587.

27   **Truman's seizures were unconstitutional:** *Youngstown*, 343 U.S. at 588.

28   **"intentional, evil deeds":** Laurence H. Tribe and Joshua Matz, *To End a Presidency: The Power of Impeachment* (Basic Books, 2018), 48.

28   **"a staunch Federalist":** "Impeachment and Trial of Justice Samuel Chase, 1804–05," US Senate, accessed May 16, 2025, https://www.senate.gov/about/powers-procedures/impeach ment/impeachment-chase.htm.

28   **asked them to impeach:** Chief Justice William Rehnquist, in a 1996 speech, dropped this delightful description: "Chase was a striking figure physically—over six feet tall, with a ruddy complexion which earned him the sobriquet (behind his back, of

course) of 'Old Bacon Face.'" Apparently, Americans in 1804 had a much better name game going than we do today. William H. Rehnquist, "The Future of the Federal Courts," speech, American University College of Law, Washington, DC, April 9, 1996, https://www.law.cornell.edu/supct/justices/rehnau96.htm.

28   **The articles of impeachment:** Rehnquist, "The Future of the Federal Courts."

29   **vice president, Aaron Burr:** Rehnquist, "The Future of the Federal Courts."

29   **outright criminal behavior:** "Impeachments of Federal Judges," Federal Judicial Center, accessed May 16, 2025, https://www.fjc.gov/history/judges/impeachments-federal-judges.

30   **the will of the people:** Rehnquist, "The Future of the Federal Courts."

30   **assessment of *Marbury v. Madison*:** "*Marbury v. Madison*."

31   **"The attacks are not random":** Josh Gerstein, "Ketanji Brown Jackson Sharply Condemns Trump's Attacks on Judges," *Politico*, May 1, 2025, https://www.politico.com/news/2025/05/01/ketanji-brown-jackson-sharply-condemns-trumps-attacks on judges 00323010.

32   **the Shakespeare quote about:** William Shakespeare, *Henry VI: Part 2*, ed. Barbara Mowat, Paul Werstine, Michael Poston, and Rebecca Niles (Folger Shakespeare Library, n.d.), accessed May 16, 2025, https://www.folger.edu/explore/shakespeares-works/henry-vi-part-2/read.

32   **German pastor Martin Niemöller:** "Martin Niemöller: 'First They Came for . . . ,'" United States Holocaust Memorial Museum, accessed May 16, 2025, https://encyclopedia.ushmm.org/content/en/article/martin-niemoeller-first-they-came-for-the-socialists.

33   **In *Federalist* 51:** Madison, *Federalist*, no. 51, 324.

CHAPTER 2: THE MYTH OF BROKEN INSTITUTIONS

36   **the thirty-four felony counts:** Ximena Bustillo and Hilary Fung, "Trump Is Found Guilty on 34 Felony Counts. Read the Counts Here," NPR, May 30, 2024, https://www.npr.org/2024/05/30/g-s1-1848/trump-hush-money-trial-34-counts.

38   **outright refusal to comply:** Peter Kafka, "Donald Trump Is Shrugging Off the Supreme Court. These Are Uncharted Waters," *Business Insider*, April 15, 2025, https://www.businessinsider.com/donald-trump-defies-supreme-court-dangerous-precedent-why-2025-4; Ashleigh Maciolek and Stephen Spaulding, "Public Statements Affirming That the President Must Comply with Court Orders," Brennan Center for Justice, February 25, 2025, https://www.brennancenter.org/our-work/research-reports/public-statements-affirming-president-must-comply-court-orders.

38   **"facilitate" Abrego Garcia's return:** Noem v. Abrego Garcia, 145 S. Ct. 1017, 1019 (2025).

39   **was delegitimizing judges:** Joyce Vance, "When They Come for the Judges," *Civil Discourse with Joyce Vance*, February 26, 2025, https://joycevance.substack.com/p/when-they-come-for-the-judges.

39   **recast as liberals:** Steve Vladeck, "Setting the Record Straight on the Anti-Trump Injunctions," *One First with Steve Vladeck*, March 31, 2025, https://www.stevevladeck.com/p/136-setting-the-record-straight-on.

40   **the language of *Federalist* 69:** Alexander Hamilton, *Federalist*, no. 69, in *The Federalist Papers*, ed. Clinton Rossiter (New American Library, 1961), 416.

41   **"the executive Power shall":** US Constitution, art. 2, sec. 1.

41   **Harvard Law professors:** Cass R. Sunstein and Adrian Vermeule, "The Unitary Executive: Past, Present, and Future,"

Supreme Court Review 2020 (2020): 83, https://www.journals
.uchicago.edu/doi/full/10.1086/714860.

42   **saw it in *Trump v. United States*:** Trump v. United States, 603
U.S. 593 (2024).

42   **backsliding democracies, such as Hungary:** Jeremy Shapiro
and Zsuzsanna Végh, "The Orbanisation of America: Hungary's Lessons for Donald Trump," European Council on Foreign Relations, October 9, 2024, https://ecfr.eu/publication
/the-orbanisation-of-america-hungarys-lessons-for-donald
-trump/.

42   **left to rot:** Taiwo Adebayo, "Children Die as USAID Aid Cuts
Snap a Lifeline for the World's Most Malnourished," Associ-
ated Press, May 15, 2025, https://apnews.com/article/usaid
-funding-cuts-humanitarian-children-trump-4447e210c4b
5543b8ebb9a6b9e01aa53.

42   **medical assistance to stay alive:** Sarah Newey, "US Aid Freeze
Claims First Victims as Oxygen Supplies Cut Off," *The Tele-
graph*, February 11, 2025, https://www.telegraph.co.uk/global
-health/climate-and-people/us-aid-freeze-claims-first
-victims-as-oxygen-supplies-cut/.

42   **Scott Detrow explained:** Scott Detrow, host, "Did the Unitary Executive Theory Pave the Way for President Trump's
Second Term?," March 23, 2025, *All Things Considered*, NPR,
https://www.npr.org/2025/03/23/nx-s1-5208112/did-the
-unitary-executive-theory-pave-the-way-for-president
-trumps-second-term.

43   **In *Federalist* 75:** Hamilton, *Federalist*, no. 75, 452.

44   **Senate Republicans turned their backs:** Andrew Glass,
"When the GOP Torpedoed Nixon," *Politico*, February 7, 2007,
https://www.politico.com/story/2007/02/when-the
-gop-torpedoed-nixon-002680.

44   **will confirm almost anyone:** Matt Gaetz was a bridge too far

and withdrew in the face of clear opposition by Senate Republicans. Eric Tucker, "Gaetz Withdraws as Trump's Nominee for Attorney General," PBS News, November 21, 2024, https://www.pbs.org/newshour/politics/florida-republican -gaetz-withdraws-as-trumps-nominee-for-attorney-general.

44 **even excellent nominees:** Ron Elving, "What Happened with Merrick Garland in 2016 and Why It Matters Now," NPR, June 29, 2018, https://www.npr.org/2018/06/29/624467256 /what-happened-with-merrick-garland-in-2016-and-why-it -matters-now.

44 **who believes habeas corpus:** Dareh Gregorian and Didi Martinez, "Homeland Security Secretary Kristi Noem Struggles to Define Habeas Corpus at Senate Hearing," NBC News, May 20, 2025, https://www.nbcnews.com/politics/immigra tion/homeland-security-secretary-kristi-noem-struggles -define-habeas-corpus-rcna207986.

45 **"It may be a reflection":** Madison, *Federalist*, no. 51, 322.

46 **Hamilton wrote in *Federalist* 73:** Hamilton, *Federalist*, no. 73, 446.

47 **In *Federalist* 78, Hamilton wrote:** Hamilton, *Federalist*, no. 78, 465–66.

47 **"writing a rule for the ages":** Trump v. United States, Docket No. 23-939, U.S. Supreme Court Oral Argument, argued April 25, 2025, transcript, 141, https://www.supremecourt.gov/oral _arguments/argument_transcripts/2023/23-939_3fb4.pdf.

48 **"now let him enforce it":** Jeffrey Rosen, "Supreme Court History: The First Hundred Years," Thirteen, PBS, accessed May 23, 2025, https://www.thirteen.org/wnet/supremecourt/ante bellum/history2.html.

48 **civil and criminal contempt powers:** Yasmin Abusaif and Douglas Keith, "What Courts Can Do If the Trump Administration Defies Court Orders," Brennan Center for Justice,

February 14, 2025, https://www.brennancenter.org/our-work
/research-reports/what-courts-can-do-if-trump-administra
tion-defies-court-orders.

48 **public's loss of confidence:** Shawn Patterson Jr. et al., "The
Withering of Public Confidence in the Courts," *Judicature* 108,
no. 1 (2024), https://judicature.duke.edu/articles/the-withering
-of-public-confidence-in-the-courts/.

49 **accepting expensive gifts:** Justin Elliott, Joshua Kaplan, and
Alex Mierjeski, "Justice Samuel Alito Took Luxury Fishing
Vacation with GOP Billionaire Who Later Had Cases before
the Court," *ProPublica*, June 20, 2023, https://www.propublica
.org/article/samuel-alito-luxury-fishing-trip-paul-singer
-scotus-supreme-court; Joshua Kaplan, Justin Elliott, and Alex
Mierjeski, "Clarence Thomas Has a Child in Private School.
Harlan Crowe Paid the Tuition," *ProPublica*, May 4, 2023,
https://www.propublica.org/article/clarence-thomas-harlan
-crow-private-school-tuition-scotus.

49 **engaging in behavior:** Jodi Kantor, Aric Toler, and Julie Tate,
"Another Provocative Flag Was Flown at Another Alito
Home," *New York Times*, May 22, 2024, https://www.nytimes
.com/2024/05/22/us/justice-alito-flag-appeal-to-heaven.html.

49 **"in the gutter":** Demand Justice, "Polling Roundup: Supreme
Court Approval Is in the Gutter. Americans Demand Reform," press release, August 8, 2024, https://demandjustice
.org/polling-roundup-supreme-court-approval-is-in-the
-gutter-americans-demand-reform/.

49 **In September 2023, Gallup concluded:** Megan Brenan, "Views
of Supreme Court Remain Near Record Lows," Gallup, September 29, 2023, https://news.gallup.com/poll/511820/views
-supreme-court-remain-near-record-lows.aspx%20/.

50 **"There is no position":** Hamilton, *Federalist*, no. 78, 467.

51 **expounded on the rationale:** Hamilton, *Federalist*, no. 78, 475.

52　**64.1 percent of eligible Americans voted:** Domenico Montanaro, "A Wild Year in Politics, by the Numbers," NPR, December 27, 2024, https://www.npr.org/2024/12/27/nx-s1-522 2570/2024-politics-recap/.

52　**second-highest level of turnout:** Montanaro, "A Wild Year in Politics."

CHAPTER 3: HOW DEMOCRACY WORKS FOR US

57　**most sarcastic of non-apologies:** "Joni Ernst Posts Sarcastic Apology for Medicaid Comments That 'We All Are Going to Die,'" *Des Moines Register*, May 31, 2025, https://www.des moinesregister.com/videos/news/politics/2025/05/31/us-sen -joni-ernst-issues-sarcastic-apology-for-medicaid-com ments/83968870007/.

58　**Winston Churchill noted:** Richard M. Langworth, "Churchill's 'Democracy Is the Worst Form of Government . . . ,'" August 1, 2024, https://richardlangworth.com/worst-form-of-govern ment.

61　**failed, but only because:** Taylor Pullins and Suzanne Knijnenburg, "US Withdrawal from the Paris Agreement: Impact and Next Steps," White & Case, January 21, 2025, https:// www.whitecase.com/insight-alert/us-withdrawal-paris -agreement-impact-and-next-steps.

61　**reupped the United States' commitment:** Matt McGrath, "US Rejoins Paris Accord: Biden's First Act Sets Tone for Ambitious Approach," BBC, February 19, 2021, https://www.bbc .com/news/science-environment-55732386.

61　**That's the value:** McGrath, "US Rejoins Paris Accord."

61　**Trump withdrew from the Paris Agreement:** Nate Perez and Rachel Waldholz, "Trump Is Withdrawing from the Paris Agreement (Again), Reversing U.S. Climate Policy,"

NPR, January 21, 2025, https://www.npr.org/2025/01/21/nx -si-5266207/trump-paris-agreement-biden-climate-change.

61 **withdraw US support:** Pullins and Knijnenburg, "US Withdrawal from the Paris Agreement."

61 **"America First Priorities":** "President Trump's America First Priorities," The White House, January 20, 2025, https://www .whitehouse.gov/briefings-statements/2025/01/president -trumps-america-first-priorities/.

62 **Trump's executive order on the subject:** "President Trump's America First Priorities."

62 **"I'm immediately withdrawing":** Perez and Waldholz, "Trump Is Withdrawing."

62 **Earlier Republican administrations:** Alec Tyson, "On Climate Change, Republicans Are Open to Some Policy Approaches, Even as They Assign the Issue Low Priority," Pew Research Center, July 23, 2021, https://www.pewresearch.org /short-reads/2021/07/23/on-climate-change-republicans-are -open-to-some-policy-approaches-even-as-they-assign-the -issue-low-priority/.

64 **register for summer school:** Jkonicek, "This Week in Universal News: The University of Alabama Is Desegregated, 1963," Unwritten Record, National Archives, June 9, 2014, https:// unwritten-record.blogs.archives.gov/2014/06/09/this-week -in-universal-news-the-university-of-alabama-is-desegre gated-1963/.

64 **James Hood was born:** Richard Goldstein, "James A. Hood, Student Who Challenged Segregation, Dies at 70," *New York Times*, January 20, 2013, https://www.nytimes.com/2013/01/21 /us/james-hood-dies-at-70-integrated-university-of-alabama .html.

64 **Hood wanted to transfer:** Goldstein, "James A. Hood."

65 **"complete mental and physical breakdown":** "James Hood,"

Through the Doors, University of Alabama, accessed May 6, 2025, https://throughthedoors.ua.edu/james-hood.html.

65 **Vivian Malone Jones stayed on campus:** "Vivian Malone Jones," Legal Defense Fund, accessed May 6, 2025, https://www.naacpldf.org/about-us/scholarship-recipients/vivian-malone-jones/.

65 **"I decided not to show any fear":** "Vivian Malone Jones."

67 **By executive order:** "Ending Radical and Wasteful Government DEI Programs and Preferencing," The White House, January 20, 2025, https://www.whitehouse.gov/presidential-actions/2025/01/ending-radical-and-wasteful-government-dei-programs-and-preferencing/.

67 **The new administration tried:** "Ending Illegal Discrimination and Restoring Merit-Based Opportunity," The White House, January 21, 2025, https://www.whitehouse.gov/presidential-actions/2025/01/ending-illegal-discrimination-and-restoring-merit-based-opportunity/.

68 **Chief Justice Roger B. Taney:** Dred Scott v. Sandford, 60 U.S. 393, 407 (1856).

69 **the Supreme Court's landmark decision:** Brown v. Board of Education of Topeka, 347 U.S. 483, 494–95 (1954).

70 **The Supreme Court failed:** Korematsu v. United States, 323 U.S. 214 (1944).

72 **The language is important:** Trump v. Hawaii, 585 U.S. 667, 710 (2018).

72 **Children's books:** Brian Niiya, "Dive into These YA Books on the Wartime Incarceration of Japanese Americans," Densho, February 21, 2021, https://densho.org/catalyst/young-adult-books-on-wartime-incarceration-of-japanese-americans.

72 **and essays:** George Takei, "George Takei: Internment, America's Great Mistake," *New York Times*, April 28, 2017, https://

www.nytimes.com/2017/04/28/opinion/george-takei
-japanese-internment-americas-great-mistake.html.

73 **"We're going back":** Sara Dorn, "Trump Cheers 'Amazing' Affirmative Action Ruling: 'What a Wonderful Day,'" *Forbes*,
June 29, 2023, https://www.forbes.com/sites/saradorn/2023
/06/29/trump-cheers-amazing-affirmative-action-ruling
-what-a-wonderful-day/.

74 **"Deeming race irrelevant in law":** Students for Fair Admissions, Inc. v. President and Fellows of Harvard College, 600
U.S. 181, 407 (2023).

74 **New Jersey Senator Cory Booker tweeted:** Cory Booker
(@CoryBooker), "If this country hasn't broken your heart, you
probably don't love Her enough," Twitter (now X), January 22,
2018, https://x.com/CoryBooker/status/955556326951866369.

75 **His opposition included:** "Participants in 'Forgotten' Teachers' March Recreate History," *Selma Times Journal*, January 22,
2015, https://www.selmatimesjournal.com/2015/01/22/partici
pants-in-forgotten-teachers-march-recreate-history/.

75 **Georgia Congressman John Lewis recounted:** "45 Years Since
Selma, Rep. John Lewis Reflects," NPR, March 8, 2010, https://
www.npr.org/2010/03/08/124461875/45-years-since-selma
-rep-john-lewis-reflects.

76 **There was also outright intimidation:** "Alabama Troopers
Attack Black People Registering to Vote in Selma," Equal Justice Initiative, accessed May 6, 2025, https://calendar.eji.org
/racial-injustice/oct/7.

76 **Then Judge Frank M. Johnson:** Jack Bass, "The Selma March
and the Judge Who Made It Happen," *Alabama Law Review* 67,
no. 2 (2015): 542, https://law.ua.edu/wp-content/uploads/2011
/07/The-Selma-March-and-the-Judge-Who-Made-It
-Happen.pdf.

77 **Johnson went on to issue court orders:** "Judge Frank M.

Johnson," National Park Service, accessed April, 26, 2025, https://www.nps.gov/people/frankmjohnsonjr.htm.

77   **"integrating, scalawagging, carpetbagging liar":** "Judge Frank M. Johnson."

77   **twenty-five thousand people strong:** "Judge Frank M. Johnson."

77   **Viola Liuzzo, a white mom:** Mary Stanton, "Viola Gregg Liuzzo," in *Encyclopedia of Alabama*, accessed April 26, 2025, https://encyclopediaofalabama.org/article/viola-gregg -liuzzo/.

78   **Dr. King said:** "Read Martin Luther King, Jr.'s 'I Have a Dream' Speech in Its Entirety," NPR, updated January 16, 2023, https:// www.npr.org/2010/01/18/122701268/i-have-a-dream-speech -in-its-entirety.

79   **"America has defaulted":** "'I Have a Dream' Speech."

79   **"the bank of justice is bankrupt":** "'I Have a Dream' Speech."

CHAPTER 4: A NEW LOST CAUSE

81   **"practically and morally responsible":** "Minority Leader McConnell Says President Trump 'Practically and Morally Responsible' for January 6 Attack on Capitol," C-SPAN, February 13, 2021, https://www.c-span.org/clip/us-senate/mino rity-leader-mcconnell-says-president-trump-practically-and -morally-responsible-for-january-6-attack-on-capitol/49 46114.

81   **"atrocious and totally wrong":** Alexander Burns and Jonathan Martin, "'I've Had It with This Guy': G.O.P. Leaders Privately Blasted Trump after Jan. 6," *New York Times*, April 21, 2022, https://www.nytimes.com/2022/04/21/us/politics/trump -mitch-mcconnell-kevin-mccarthy.html%20/.

82   **But their outrage:** Sonam Sheth, "Full List of Republicans

Breaking with Trump on January 6 Pardons," *Newsweek*, January 21, 2025, https://www.newsweek.com/full-list-republi cans-criticizing-trump-january-6-pardons-2018618.

82   **my real-time assessment:** Joyce Vance, "The Pro-Trump Insurrection at the Capitol Is Over. The Threat Posed by Its Leaders Isn't," MSNBC, January 8, 2021, https://www.msnbc .com/opinion/pro-trump-insurrection-capitol-over-threat -posed-its-leaders-isn-n1253585.

82   **to prosecute every case:** Dan Mangan, "Federal Prosecutor Doesn't Rule Out Charging Trump for Inciting Capitol Riot," CNBC, January 7, 2021, https://www.cnbc.com/2021 /01/07/federal-prosecutor-doesnt-rule-out-prosecuting-trump -for-inciting-capitol-riot.html.

83   **Proclamation of Amnesty and Reconstruction:** Abraham Lincoln, "Proclamation of Amnesty and Reconstruction," December 8, 1863, Abraham Lincoln papers: Series 1, General Correspondence, 1833 to 1916 (manuscript / mixed material), https://www.loc.gov/item/mal2849300/.

84   **they remained law-abiding:** "Surrender Documents," April 9, 1865, Appomattox Court House, National Park Service, accessed May 30, 2025, https://www.nps.gov/apco/learn/histo ryculture/surrender-documents.htm.

84   **at least three people:** "Slaves of Andrew Johnson," National Park Service, accessed May 30, 2025, https://www.nps.gov /anjo/learn/historyculture/slaves.htm.

84   **ready to issue universal amnesty:** "President Andrew Johnson Pardons Confederate John C. Shelton, 1866," Document Bank of Virginia, Library of Virginia, accessed May 30, 2025, https://edu.lva.virginia.gov/dbva/items/show/149.

84   **"prudential reservations and exceptions":** Andrew Johnson, "Proclamation 179—Granting Full Pardon and Amnesty for the Offense of Treason against the United States during the

Late Civil War," December 25, 1868, American Presidency Project, accessed May 30, 2025, https://www.presidency.ucsb .edu/documents/proclamation-179-granting-full-pardon -and-amnesty-for-the-offense-treason-against-the.

85 **"tend to secure permanent peace":** Johnson, "Proclamation 179."

85 **Jefferson Davis went to prison:** Jim Flook, "Jefferson Davis's Imprisonment," in *Encyclopedia Virginia* (Virginia Humanities, December 7, 2020), https://encyclopediavirginia.org/en tries/jefferson-daviss-imprisonment/.

85 **oath of loyalty:** Andrew Glass, "House Votes to Restore Citizenship to Gen. Robert E. Lee, July 22, 1975," *Politico*, July 22, 2018, https://www.politico.com/story/2018/07/22/this-day-in -politics-july-22-1975-724528.

86 **list of generals:** Michael Bezilla, "Historian Explores How Civil War Northerners Reconciled Treason with Leniency," Penn State, June 30, 2014, https://www.psu.edu/news/research /story/historian-explores-how-civil-war-northerners -reconciled-treason-leniency.

86 **"counterfeit varnish of patriotism":** William A. Blair, *With Malice Toward Some: Treason and Loyalty in the Civil War Era* (University of North Carolina Press, 2014), 309.

87 **Edward Alfred Pollard:** "Edward Alfred Pollard," National Park Service, accessed May 30, 2025, https://www.nps.gov /people/edward-alfred-pollard.htm.

88 **Trump was acquitted 57–43:** Wendy Leonard, "Why Romney Voted to Convict and Lee Voted to Acquit Trump in 2nd Impeachment Trial," *Deseret News*, February 13, 2021, https:// www.deseret.com/utah/2021/2/13/22281675/why-mitt -romney-voted-to-convict-trump-in-the-former-presidents -2nd-impeachment-trial/.

88 **a reference to the impeachment:** Chris Cillizza, "An Incredibly

Damning Quote from Mitch McConnell on January 6," CNN, April 21, 2022, https://www.cnn.com/2022/04/21/politics/mitch -mcconnell-january-trump/index.html.

88 **should hold Trump accountable:** Ryan Goodman and Josh Asabor, "In Their Own Words: The 43 Republicans' Explanations of Their Votes Not to Convict Trump in Impeachment Trial," Just Security, February 15, 2021, https://www.justsecu rity.org/74725/in-their-own-words-the-43-republicans -explanations-of-their-votes-not-to-convict-trump-in -impeachment-trial/.

88 **take care of Trump:** Julie Tsirkin et al., "McConnell Tells GOP Colleagues He Will Vote to Acquit Trump," February 13, 2021, NBC News, https://www.nbcnews.com/politics/donald -trump/mcconnell-tells-gop-colleagues-he-will-vote-acquit -trump-n1257823.

88 **a different idea:** Trump v. United States, 603 U.S. 593 (2024).

88 **try a *former* president:** Chuck Grassley, "Grassley Statement on Impeachment Trial," press release, February 13, 2021, https://www.grassley.senate.gov/news/news-releases/grass ley-statement-on-impeachment-trial; Kevin Cramer, "Sen. Cramer Statement on Voting to Acquit Former President Trump," press release, February 13, 2021, https://www.cramer .senate.gov/news/press-releases/sen-cramer-statement -on-voting-to-acquit-former-president-trump; John Thune, "Thune Statement on Conclusion of Senate Impeachment Trial," press release, February 13, 2021, https://www.thune .senate.gov/public/index.cfm/press-releases?ID=879F5D24 -FCCD-49F0-8E57-E7604722BC09.

88 **Utah Senator Mike Lee:** "Senator Mike Lee Deems Impeachment Process as 'Politically Suspicious,' Shares Thoughts on Trump's Acquittal," ABC 4, February 13, 2021, https://www .abc4.com/news/local-news/senator-mike-lee-deems

-impeachment-trial-as-politically-suspicious-shares
-thoughts-on-trumps-acquittal/.

88   **Republicans pushed for the delay:** Mike DeBonis and Seung Min Kim, "Top Senate Republicans Push to Delay Trump Impeachment Trial," *Washington Post*, January 21, 2021, https:// www.washingtonpost.com/politics/senate-repulicans-delay -impeachment-trial/2021/01/21/4eb54eee-5c0c-11eb-b8bd -ee36b1cd18bf_story.html.

89   **"We nearly lost America":** Joe Biden, "Remarks by President Biden on the Third Anniversary of the January 6th Attack and Defending the Sacred Cause of American Democracy," Montgomery County Community College, Blue Bell, PA, January 5, 2024, https://bidenwhitehouse.archives.gov/briefing -room/speeches-remarks/2024/01/05/remarks-by-president -biden-on-the-third-anniversary-of-the-january-6th-attack -and-defending-the-sacred-cause-of-american-democracy -blue-bell-pa/.

89   **4chan and other sites:** Aruna Viswanatha and Sadie Gurman, "Ahead of Capitol Riot, Police Miscalculated Risk," *Wall Street Journal*, January 8, 2021, https://www.wsj.com/politics /elections/actions-by-police-before-trump-supporters -attacked-capitol-backfired-spectacularly-11610064600.

90   **As FDR said in 1941:** "President Franklin Roosevelt's Annual Message (Four Freedoms) to Congress (1941)," National Archives, January 6, 1941, https://www.archives.gov/milestone -documents/president-franklin-roosevelts-annual-message -to-congress.

91   **2010 book, *The Rule of Law*:** Tom Bingham, *The Rule of Law* (Penguin Books, 2010).

91   **"People value the Rule of Law":** Jeremy Waldron, "The Rule of Law," in *The Stanford Encyclopedia of Philosophy*, ed. Edward

N. Zalta and Uri Nodelman (Stanford University, Fall 2023 edition), https://plato.stanford.edu/entries/rule-of-law/.

92 **"ideals of our political morality":** Waldron, "The Rule of Law."

92 **control of his business interests:** "President Trump's 3,400 Conflicts of Interest," Citizens for Responsibility and Ethics in Washington, September 24, 2020, https://www.citizens forethics.org/reports-investigations/crew-reports/president -trumps-3400-conflicts-of-interest/.

92 **Emoluments Clauses of the Constitution:** Gabe Lezra, "Profiting off the Presidency: Trump's Violations of the Emoluments Clauses," American Constitution Society for Law and Policy, October 1, 2019, https://www.acslaw.org/expertforum /profiting-off-the-presidency-trumps-violations-of-the -emoluments-clauses/.

92 **violate the Hatch Act:** "OSC Issues Hatch Act Report Documenting Violations by 13 Senior Trump Administration Officials, Including at the 2020 Republican National Convention," press release, U.S. Office of Special Counsel, November 9, 2021, https://osc.gov/News/Pages/21-02-Hatch-Act-Report-RNC .aspx; Josh Wagner and Michelle Ye Hee Lee, "Trump Says He Won't Fire Kellyanne Conway over Hatch Act Violations," *Washington Post*, June 14, 2019, https://www.washingtonpost .com/politics/trump-says-he-wont-fire-kellyanne-conway -over-hatch-act-violations/2019/06/14/76f31a94-8e9f-11e9 -adf3-f70f78c156e8_story.html.

92 **can bring the full power:** Michael C. Bender, Alan Blinder, and Jonathan Swan, "Inside Trump's Pressure Campaign on Universities," *New York Times*, April 14, 2025, https://www.ny times.com/2025/04/14/us/politics/trump-pressure-univer sities.html; Daniel Ortner, "Trump's Attack on Law Firms Threatens the Foundations of Our Justice System," Foundation for Individual Rights and Expression, March 18, 2025, https: //www.thefire.org/news/trumps-attack-law-firms-threatens

-foundations-our-justice-system; David Smith, "Trump Orders DOJ to Investigate Two Former Officials Who Defied Him," *The Guardian*, April 9, 2025, https://www.theguardian.com/us-news/2025/apr/09/trump-justice-department-critics; Miranda Jeyaretnam, "These Are the Students Targeted by Trump's Immigration Enforcement over Campus Activism," *Time*, April 1, 2025, https://time.com/7272060/international-students-targeted-trump-ice-detention-deport-campus-palestinian-activism/; Hugo Lowell, "Trump Personally Ordered Firings of Special Counsel Prosecutors," *The Guardian*, February 4, 2025, https://www.theguardian.com/us-news/2025/feb/04/trump-jack-smith-special-counsel-prosecutors-firings; Maegan Vazquez, "Trump, White House Lash Out at Judge Who Ruled on Deporting Migrants to South Sudan," *Washington Post*, May 22, 2025, https://www.washingtonpost.com/politics/2025/05/22/trump-criticizes-judge-sudan-deportation/.

93 **"established standing laws":** John Locke, *Two Treatises of Government* (G. Routledge and Sons, 1632–1704), sec. 131.

95 **George Orwell wrote:** George Orwell, *1984* (Planet eBook, 1949), 197.

95 **Atwood has said:** Margaret Atwood, "I Invented Gilead. The Supreme Court Is Making It Real," *The Atlantic*, May 13, 2022, https://www.theatlantic.com/ideas/archive/2022/05/supreme-court-roe-handmaids-tale-abortion-margaret-atwood/629833/.

96 **threat—declining fertility:** A concern that is actually being voiced in 2025. Isabel van Brugen, "Elon Musk Issues Birth Rate Warning for US," *Newsweek*, April 22, 2025, https://www.newsweek.com/elon-musk-birth-rate-warning-us-2062571#:~:text=Musk%2C%2053%2C%20the%20CEO%20of,boosting%20fertility%20and%20population%20research.

96   **The dangerous vice:** James Madison, *Federalist*, no. 10, in *The Federalist Papers*, ed. Clinton Rossiter (New American Library, 1961), 78.

98   **"delegation of the government":** Madison, *Federalist*, no. 10, 82.

98   **"a happy combination":** Madison, *Federalist*, no. 10, 91.

100   **This led him to conclude:** Madison, *Federalist*, no. 10, 92.

101   **back to Orwell:** Orwell, *1984*, 102.

102   **"It's illegal," King said:** Angus King, "King to Senate Colleagues: 'We've Got to Wake Up [and] Protect This Institution,'" press release, February 10, 2025, https://www.king.senate .gov/newsroom/press-releases/king-to-senate-colleagues -weve-got-to-wake-up-and-protect-this-institution/.

102   **His words bear careful reading:** King, "'We've Got to Wake Up.'"

104   **flunked out of grammar school:** "Interesting Facts about Thomas Paine," Boston Tea Party Ships & Museum, accessed June 21, 2025, https://www.bostonteapartyship.com/thomas -paine-facts.

104   **"a failure at all":** "The Founding Failure," From the Green Notebook, January 30, 2018, https://fromthegreennotebook .com/2018/01/30/the-founding-failure/.

104   **he published *Common Sense*:** "Thomas Paine Publishes 'Common Sense,'" History.com, last modified February 18, 2025, https://www.history.com/this-day-in-history/january-10 /thomas-paine-publishes-common-sense.

104   **half a million copies:** "Thomas Paine: The Original Publishing Viral Superstar," National Constitution Center, January 10, 2023, https://constitutioncenter.org/blog/thomas-paine -the-original-publishing-viral-superstar-2.

104   **one in five Americans:** Sanjoy Mahajan, "Were Colonial

Americans More Literate Than Americans Today?," Freako-
nomics, September 1, 2011, https://freakonomics.com/2011
/09/were-colonial-americans-more-literate-than-americans
-today/.

104 **read aloud in neighborhood pubs:** "Thomas Paine."

104 **"The Cause of America":** Thomas Paine, *Common Sense: Addressed to the Inhabitants of America on the Following Subjects*
(1776).

104 **"power to begin the world":** Paine, *Common Sense.*

105 **"that try men's souls":** Thomas Paine, *The American Crisis*
(1776).

105 **the weaknesses of kings:** Paine, *Common Sense.*

105 **"LONG LIVE THE KING!":** Donald J. Trump (@realDon-
aldTrump), "CONGESTION PRICING IS DEAD. Manhattan,
and all of New York, is SAVED. LONG LIVE THE KING!,"
Truth Social, February 19, 2025, https://truthsocial.com/@real
DonaldTrump/posts/114032082899254855.

106 **Trump wearing a golden crown:** The White House
(@WhiteHouse), "'CONGESTION PRICING IS DEAD. Man-
hattan, and all of New York, is SAVED. LONG LIVE THE
KING!'—President Donald J. Trump," X (formerly Twitter),
February 19, 2025, https://x.com/WhiteHouse/status/189229
5984928993698.

106 **wrote, "most ignorant and unfit":** Paine, *Common Sense.*

106 **Paine reasoned that:** Paine, *Common Sense.*

107 *The American Crisis begins:* Paine, *American Crisis.*

107 **McCarthyism and the "Red Scare":** "McCarthyism / The 'Red
Scare,'" Dwight D. Eisenhower Presidential Library, Museum
& Boyhood Home, accessed May 31, 2025, https://www.eisen
howerlibrary.gov/research/online-documents/mccarthyism
-red-scare.

108 **Eisenhower avoided confrontation:** "McCarthyism and the Red Scare," UVA Miller Center, accessed May 31, 2025, https:// millercenter.org/the-presidency/educational-resources/age -of-eisenhower/mcarthyism-red-scare.

108 **Early in 1954:** "Have You No Sense of Decency?," US Senate, June 9, 1954, https://www.senate.gov/about/powers-proce dures/investigations/mccarthy-hearings/have-you-no-sense -of-decency.htm.

108 **Senate records tell the story:** "Have You No Sense of Decency?"

109 **will be on the ballot:** "United States Congressional Elections, 2026," Ballotpedia, accessed May 31, 2025, https://ballotpedia .org/United_States_Congress_elections,_2026.

CHAPTER 5: RBG'S UMBRELLA

112 **as the "illiberal democracy":** Matt Apuzzo and Benjamin Novak, "In Hungary, Viktor Orban Remakes an Election to His Liking," *New York Times*, March 31, 2022, https://www.ny times.com/2022/03/31/world/europe/hungary-viktor-orban -election.html%20/.

112 **dead or imprisoned:** Laura Gozzi and Francis Scarr, "Russian Election: Why Putin's Fifth Term as President Was Never in Doubt," BBC, March 17, 2024, https://www.bbc.com/news /world-europe-68505228; Angela Stent, "The Death of Alexei Navalny," Brookings Institution, February 16, 2024, https:// www.brookings.edu/articles/the-death-of-alexei-navalny/.

115 **the original foot soldiers:** Joyce Vance (@joyce_white_vance), "George Sallie, foot soldier from the original Selma march & proud voter. He still comes out every year to commemorate the violence he & his community endured to gain the right to vote. By voting in every election, I honor him & his sacrifice.

Hero.," Instagram, March 4, 2020, https://www.instagram
.com/p/B9VlpvlJaDc/; George McDonald, "Selma Foot Soldiers Meet President Biden during Jubilee," WAKA 8 Action News, March 10, 2023, https://www.waka.com/2023/03/10
/selma-foot-soldiers-meet-president-biden-during-jubilee/.

116 **"hit upside the head":** Brady Talbert, "Historian, Community
Leaders React to Death of Selma Foot Soldier," WSFA 12, January 22, 2024, https://www.wsfa.com/2024/01/23/historian
-community-leaders-react-death-selma-foot-soldier/.

117 **often attributed to Thomas Jefferson:** "Government by the
Majority Who Participate (Spurious Quotation)," Monticello,
accessed June 2, 2025, https://www.monticello.org/research
-education/thomas-jefferson-encyclopedia/government
-majority-who-participate-spurious-quotation/.

117 **President George W. Bush said:** George W. Bush, "Fact Sheet:
Voting Rights Act Reauthorization and Amendments Act of
2006," press release, July 26, 2006, https://georgewbush-white
house.archives.gov/news/releases/2006/07/20060727-1.html.

118 **The reauthorization Bush signed:** Bush, "Fact Sheet."

118 **of the act, Section 5:** 52 U.S.C. § 10304.

118 **decided *Shelby County v. Holder*:** Shelby County, Ala. v. Holder,
570 U.S. 529 (2013).

118 **majority opinion in *Shelby County*:** *Shelby County*, 570 U.S. at
547–48.

119 **with prescient clarity:** *Shelby County*, 570 U.S. at 590 (Ginsburg, J., dissenting).

119 ***Citizens United v. Federal Election Commission*:** Citizens United
v. Fed. Election Comm'n, 558 U.S. 310 (2010).

121 **date the voter fraud narrative:** Michael Wines, "How Charges
of Voter Fraud Became a Political Strategy," *New York
Times*, October 21, 2016, https://www.nytimes.com/2016/10

/22/us/how-charges-of-voter-fraud-became-a-political-strategy.html.

121 **fewer than ten cases:** Natasha Khan and Corbin Carson, "Comprehensive Database of U.S. Voter Fraud Uncovers No Evidence That Photo ID Is Needed," News 21, August 12, 2012, https://votingrights.news21.com/article/election-fraud/.

122 **only thirty-one credible claims:** Justin Levitt, "A Comprehensive Investigation of Voter Impersonation Finds 31 Credible Incidents out of One Billion Ballots Cast," *Washington Post*, August 6, 2014, https://www.washingtonpost.com/news/wonk/wp/2014/08/06/a-comprehensive-investigation-of-voter-impersonation-finds-31-credible-incidents-out-of-one-billion-ballots-cast/.

122 **it is very rare:** Levitt, "A Comprehensive Investigation."

122 **outcome of our elections remain unproven:** Wines, "How Charges of Voter Fraud Became a Political Strategy."

122 **That's because it's a myth:** "The Myth of Voter Fraud," Brennan Center for Justice, accessed June 2, 2025, https://www.brennancenter.org/issues/ensure-every-american-can-vote/vote-suppression/myth-voter-fraud.

122 *claims* **of voter fraud:** Walter Olson, "'Lost, Not Stolen': Prominent Conservatives Refute 2020 Election Myths," Cato Institute, July 21, 2022, https://www.cato.org/blog/lost-not-stolen-prominent-conservatives-refute-2020-election-myths.

122 **a noncitizen waiting to vote:** Michael Waldman, "Why the Myth of Noncitizen Voting Persists," Brennan Center for Justice, August 21, 2024, https://www.brennancenter.org/our-work/analysis-opinion/why-myth-noncitizen-voting-persists.

122 **people are being bused:** Robert Farley, "No Evidence of Busing Voters to N.H.," FactCheck, February 14, 2017, https://

www.factcheck.org/2017/02/no-evidence-of-busing
-voters-to-n-h/.

122 **study after study confirms:** Elaine Kamarck, "How Wide-
spread Is Election Fraud in the United States? Not Very,"
Brookings Institution, October 28, 2024, https://www.brook
ings.edu/articles/how-widespread-is-election-fraud-in
-the-united-states-not-very/; Ashley Lopez, "How We Know
Voter Fraud Is Very Rare in U.S. Elections," NPR, October
11, 2024, https://www.npr.org/2024/10/11/nx-s1-5147732/voter
-fraud-explainer.

123 **voted in 2018, 2020, and 2022:** Hannah Hartig et al., *Republi-
can Gains in 2022 Midterms Driven Mostly by Turnout Advantage*
(Pew Research Center, 2023), 11, https://www.pewresearch.org
/politics/2023/07/12/voter-turnout-2018-2022/; "United States
Voter Turnout," University of Florida Election Lab, accessed
June 2, 2025, https://election.lab.ufl.edu/voter-turnout/.

123 **eligible voters stayed home:** Hartig et al., *Turnout Advantage*, 11.

123 **51 percent of Americans didn't:** Hartig et al., *Turnout Advantage*, 11.

123 **Approximately 36 percent didn't:** "2024 General Election
Turnout," University of Florida Election Lab, accessed June 2,
2025, https://election.lab.ufl.edu/2024-general-election-turn
out/.

124 **The National Voter Registration Act:** "The National Voter
Registration Act of 1993 (NVRA)," US Department of Justice,
accessed June 3, 2025, https://www.justice.gov/crt/national
-voter-registration-act-1993-nvra.

125 **gave an interview:** Mark Joseph Stern, "Alabama Secretary of
State: Helping More People Vote Would 'Cheapen the Work'
of Civil Rights Heroes," *Slate*, November 2, 2016, https://slate
.com/news-and-politics/2016/11/alabama-secretary-of-state

-says-more-voting-would-cheapen-the-work-of-civil-rights
-heroes.html.

125 **voting as a "privilege":** Stern, "Alabama Secretary of State."

125 **Safeguard American Voter Eligibility (SAVE) Act:** SAVE Act,
H.R. 22, 119th Cong. (2025).

125 **The second was an executive order:** "Preserving and Protecting the Integrity of American Elections," The White
House, March 25, 2025, https://www.whitehouse.gov/presi
dential-actions/2025/03/preserving-and-protecting-the
-integrity-of-american-elections/.

126 **at least twenty-one million Americans:** Kevin Morris and
Cora Henry, "Millions of Americans Don't Have Documents
Proving Their Citizenship Readily Available," Brennan Center for Justice, June 11, 2024, https://www.brennancenter.org
/our-work/analysis-opinion/millions-americans-dont-have
-documents-proving-their-citizenship-readily.

126 **Only 51 percent:** Nathan Diller, "Americans Want to See the
World, but Only 51% Took This Important Step to Do It,"
USA Today, October 23, 2024, https://www.usatoday.com
/story/travel/news/2024/10/23/state-department-issues
-record-us-passports/75794556007/.

126 **trained to run checks:** "Legislative Approaches to Ensuring Only Citizens Vote," National Conference of State
Legislatures, May 12, 2025, https://www.ncsl.org/elections
-and-campaigns/legislative-approaches-to-ensuring-only
-citizens-vote.

126 **it's a crime:** Omnibus Consolidated Appropriations Act, 1997,
Pub. L. No. 104-208, 110 Stat. 3009 (1996).

126 **on voting were uncertain:** "League of Women Voters v.
Trump," Brennan Center for Justice, June 2, 2025, https://

www.brennancenter.org/our-work/court-cases/league
-women-voters-v-trump.

126 **similar measures under consideration:** Matt Cohen, "The
SAVE Act Faces an Uphill Battle. But Some States Want to Impose Similar Measures," Democracy Docket, April 29, 2025,
https://www.democracydocket.com/news-alerts/the-save
-act-faces-an-uphill-battle-but-some-states-want-to-impose
-similar-measures/.

127 **"pruned" from the voter rolls:** "Voter Rolls and Voter Purging:
An Explainer," Rock the Vote, September 22, 2022, https://www
.rockthevote.org/explainers/voter-rolls-and-voter-purging
-an-explainer/; "Voter Purges," Brennan Center for Justice, accessed June 4, 2025, https://www.brennancenter.org/issues/en
sure-every-american-can-vote/vote-suppression/voter-purges.

127 *Husted v. A. Philip Randolph Institute*: Husted v. A. Philip
Randolph Inst., 584 U.S. 756 (2018).

131 **extreme voter suppression efforts:** Alexa Ura, "Texas' Oldest
Black University Was Built on a Former Plantation. Its Students Still Fight a Legacy of Voter Suppression," *Texas Tribune*,
February 25, 2021, https://www.texastribune.org/2021/02/25
/waller-county-texas-voter-suppression/.

133 **90 million of the 245 million:** Alan Kronenberg, "How Many
People Didn't Vote in the 2024 Election?," *U.S. News and World
Report*, November 15, 2024, https://www.usnews.com/news
/national-news/articles/2024-11-15/how-many-people-didnt
-vote-in-the-2024-election.

133 **only 37 percent voted:** Hartig et al., *Turnout Advantage*, 11.

134 **13 percent of those:** "State-by-State Youth Voter Turnout
Data and the Impact of Election Laws in 2022," Tufts Center
for Information & Research on Civic Learning and Engage-
ment, April 6, 2023, https://circle.tufts.edu/latest-research

/state-state-youth-voter-turnout-data-and-impact-election-laws-2022.

135   **In her dissenting opinion:** *Shelby County*, 570 U.S. at 581–82 (Ginsburg, J., dissenting).

CHAPTER 6: WE ARE THE CAVALRY

139   **"The simple step":** Jonathan Glover and M. J. Scott-Taggart, "It Makes No Difference Whether I Do It or Not," *Proceedings of the Aristotelian Society, Supplementary Volumes*, vol. 49 (1975): 184, https://www.jstor.org/stable/4106873.

144   **Finland developed a campaign:** Jenny Gross, "How Finland Is Teaching a Generation to Spot Misinformation," *New York Times*, January 10, 2023, https://www.nytimes.com/2023/01/10/world/europe/finland-misinformation-classes.html.

144   **resilience in fighting misinformation:** Marin Lessenski, "How It Started, How It Is Going: Media Literacy Index 2022," Open Society Institute Sofia, October 12, 2022, https://osis.bg/?p=4243&lang=en.

144   **expanded into adult education:** Gross, "How Finland Is Teaching a Generation to Spot Misinformation."

150   **the young musicians:** Scott Pelley, "What Musicians Did After an Executive Order on DEI Led to the Cancellation of U.S. Marine Band Collaboration," CBS News, March 16, 2025, https://www.cbsnews.com/news/concert-cancellation-trump-administration-dei-order-60-minutes-transcript/.

150   **Former band members:** Pelley, "What Musicians Did."

152   **As President Reagan said:** Ronald Reagan, "Ronald Reagan's Speech to Chamber of Commerce Annual Meeting in Phoenix, Arizona (Subject: Encroaching Control)," March 30, 1961, Ronald Reagan Presidential Library & Museum, https://www.reaganlibrary.gov/archives/audio/ronald-reagans-speech

-chamber-commerce-annual-meeting-phoenix-arizona
-subject.

152 **put it more succinctly:** Joseph R. Biden Jr., "A Proclamation
on Veterans Day, 2024," The White House, November 6, 2024,
https://bidenwhitehouse.archives.gov/briefing-room/presi
dential-actions/2024/11/06/a-proclamation-on-veterans-day
-2024/.

153 **Eisenhower wrote in his proclamation:** Dwight D. Eisenhower, "Proclamation 3221—Law Day, 1958," *Federal Register*
23, no. 27 (February 7, 1958): 821, https://www.govinfo.gov
/content/pkg/FR-1958-02-07/pdf/FR-1958-02-07.pdf.

157 **president characterized as pro-Trump:** Maciej Martewicz
and Agnieszka Barteczko, "Nationalist Wins Poland's Presidency in Setback for EU Ties," Bloomberg, June 2, 2025,
https://www.bloomberg.com/news/articles/2025-06-01/pol
ish-nationalist-moves-ahead-in-president-vote-new-poll
-shows.

157 **most promising way:** E. Doyle Stevick, *How Can Schools Promote Rule of Law Norms in Transitioning Societies? Lessons from
Post-Communist Europe* (JUSTRAC, 2019), https://justrac.org
/wp-content/uploads/2019/04/Stevick-How-Can-Schools
-Promote-Rule-of-Law-Norms-in-Transitioning-Societies.pdf.

157 **Stevick writes that:** Stevick, *How Can Schools Promote Rule of
Law Norms*, ii.

158 **Law Day speech in 1958:** Charles S. Rhyne, "Law Day Speech
for Voice of America," Washington, DC, May 1, 1958, Pennsylvania Bar Association, https://www.pabar.org/public/educa
tion/lawday/Rhyne-Speech.PDF.

158 **Law Day in May 2000:** Marie-Louise H. Bernal, "Law Day
2000," *Library of Congress Information Bulletin* 59, no. 6 (2000),
https://www.loc.gov/loc/lcib/0006/lawday.html.

160 **Canceling celebrations of:** Ken Dilanian et al., "Federal Agencies Bar Black History Month and Other 'Special Observances,'" NBC News, January 31, 2025, https://www.nbcnews.com/politics/donald-trump/defense-agency-bans-black-history-month-rcna190189.

160 **the work of women:** Caitlyn Burchett, "Pentagon Moves to Cancel 'Woke' Women in National Security Program Established during Trump's First Term," *Stars and Stripes*, April 29, 2025, https://www.stripes.com/theaters/us/2025-04-29/hegseth-women-peace-security-act%C2%A0woke-trump-17623674.html; Patricia Kime, "Army, Navy Pull Down Web Pages Devoted to Women in Military," Military.com, February 6, 2025, https://www.military.com/daily-news/2025/02/06/army-navy-pull-down-web-pages-devoted-women-military-service.html.

160 **Defense Department may have halted:** Will Steakin and Matt Seyler, "Pentagon Intelligence Agency Pauses Events, Activities Related to MLK Day, Black History Month," ABC News, January 29, 2025, https://abcnews.go.com/Politics/pentagon-intelligence-agency-pauses-events-activities-related-mlk/story?id=118244237.

CONCLUSION

164 **anti-immigrant bill in 2011:** United States v. Alabama, 813 F. Supp. 2d 1282 (N.D. Ala. 2011).

POSTSCRIPT

167 *Trump v. CASA,* **stalled**: Trump v. CASA, Inc., 606 U.S. no. 24A884 (2025).

169 **"what a democracy is about":** "In Forceful Senate Floor Speech, Senator Murray Slams Trump Administration for Aggres-

sively Detaining Senator Padilla at Public Press Conference,"
Office of US Senator Patty Murray, June 12, 2025, https://
www.murray.senate.gov/in-forceful-senate-floor-speech
-senator-murray-slams-trump-administration-for-aggres
sively-detaining-senator-padilla-at-public-press-conference/.

169   **victim-blaming Padilla:** Stef W. Kight and Andrew Solender,
"Republicans Are All Over the Place on Alex Padilla's Forcible
Removal," Axios, June 12, 2025, https://www.axios.com/2025
/06/12/republicans-alex-padilla-detained-video.

171   **"want to go hiking":** "Fact-checking Trump's Remarks at 'Alligator Alcatraz' on Immigration and Medicaid," PBS.org, July
2, 2025, https://www.pbs.org/newshour/politics/fact
-checking-trumps-remarks-at-alligator-alcatraz-on-immi
gration-and-medicaid.

171   **may take a concrete experience:** Jack Healy, "A Missouri
Town Was Solidly Behind Trump. Then Carol Was Detained,"
New York Times, May 29, 2025, https://www.nytimes.com/2025
/05/28/us/missouri-immigrant-trump.html; Nathan Solis,
"9-Year-Old Torrance Elementary Student Deported with
Father to Honduras," *Los Angeles Times*, June 11, 2025, https:
//www.latimes.com/california/story/2025-06-11/torrance
-boy-father-deported-honduras; Adam Goldman, "As Oust-
ers Continue, F.B.I. Singles Out Employee over Friendship
with Trump Critic," *New York Times*, June 5, 2025, https:
//www.nytimes.com/2025/06/05/us/politics/fbi-agents-patel
-trump.html.

About the Author

J oyce Vance is the former U.S. Attorney for the Northern District of Alabama, an office she held during the Obama administration. She resigned on the eve of Donald Trump's first inauguration, after twenty-five years of service as a career federal prosecutor. Vance is a Distinguished Professor of the Practice of Law at the University of Alabama School of Law. She is a legal analyst for NBC and MSNBC, the author of the popular "Civil Discourse" Substack, and the cohost of two podcasts: *#SistersInLaw* and *Cafe*'s *Insider*. She lives in Birmingham, Alabama, with her husband, Bob, a retired judge, and a menagerie of children, chickens, cats, and dogs.